MW00940090

Pocket Languages

Dutch
Pocket
Puzzles

The Basics
Volume 2

Compiled by Erik Zidowecki

Note: In some cases , the common word for something may be used instead of the formal word, so as to help provide you with a more natural vocabulary.

For more language learning materials and the chance to meet other language learners, visit http://www.parleremo.org

Part of the Pocket Languages series.
Published by Scriveremo Publishing, a division of Parleremo Languages.

ISBN-13: 978-1545487044
ISBN-10: 1545487049

This book has activities in 8 themes of vocabulary:

Animals   **Days, Months, Seasons**
Around the House **Family**
Clothing   **Numbers**
Colours   **Parts of the Body**

Contents

Welcome to the
Word Search section!

Find all the Dutch words in the puzzles.

Words may be in any direction vertically, horizontally and diagonally.

Parts of speech are given in [].

m = masculine noun

f = feminine noun

mf = masculine / feminine noun

n = neuter noun

adj = adjective

num = number

mp = masculine plural

fp = feminine plural

mfp = masculine / feminine plural

np = neuter plural

adv = adverb

v = verb

Word Search #1 - Animals

```
k  a  d  n  a  p  t  d  y  w  p  e  j  b  o  a  r
m  s  l  a  m  a  n  a  a  i  v  a  b  h  y  o  p
w  a  n  g  z  a  k  e  e  k  h  o  o  r  n  e  p
b  m  r  s  t  i  n  k  d  i  e  r  y  i  s  o  v
b  u  i  a  u  k  r  w  c  c  d  p  s  c  r  g  e
c  i  h  h  d  e  j  o  n  r  o  o  h  s  u  e  n
y  s  z  g  i  a  t  l  d  r  a  a  p  i  u  l  j
d  w  v  t  e  t  z  f  g  a  z  e  l  l  e  i  w
n  s  s  x  a  n  s  p  f  w  a  s  p  f  o  w  k
r  o  v  k  w  h  i  a  i  d  r  a  a  p  v  e  p
```

Dutch	English
kat *[m]*	cat
wangzakeekhoorn *[m]*	chipmunk
luipaard *[n]*	leopard
stier *[m]*	bull
gazelle *[f]*	gazelle
baviaan *[m]*	baboon
stinkdier *[n]*	squirrel
neushoorn *[m]*	rhinoceros
lama *[m]*	llama
wolf *[m]*	wolf
panda *[m]*	panda
vos *[m]*	fox
paard *[n]*	horse
muis *[f]*	mouse

Word Search #2 - Animals

```
x  a  d  n  a  p  c  p  o  f  g  n  a  l  s  t  p
k  o  n  i  j  n  y  a  w  o  l  f  c  v  r  y  z
j  a  c  h  t  l  u  i  p  a  a  r  d  e  z  x  z
r  a  n  e  l  e  z  i  y  x  d  s  h  j  v  f  s
e  a  i  s  h  b  n  r  o  o  h  s  u  e  n  j  f
i  m  w  a  n  g  z  a  k  e  e  k  h  o  o  r  n
d  k  w  s  t  j  t  i  j  g  e  r  p  v  y  u  z
r  o  d  e  l  y  n  x  j  u  j  v  i  l  j  r  g
i  b  d  t  h  h  h  g  r  e  i  t  s  n  h  v  i
k  g  g  m  r  n  v  o  s  f  l  b  e  e  r  n  s
```

Dutch	English
wangzakeekhoorn *[m]*	chipmunk
stier *[m]*	bull
vos *[m]*	fox
jachtluipaard *[n]*	cheetah
panda *[m]*	panda
wolf *[m]*	wolf
rode lynx *[m]*	bobcat
tijger *[m]*	tiger
dier *[n]*	animal
hert *[n]*	deer
neushoorn *[m]*	rhinoceros
beer *[m]*	bear
konijn *[n]*	rabbit
slang *[m]*	snake

Word Search #3 - Animals

```
m b c t h i d a s j p l a m a d l
e s t i e r m d p z a x y d u r n
i o w e f f a r i g v h o n p a g
d r a a p i u l t h c a j v x a o
s p d o d h v a r k e n g s d p r
d k x v t n a f i l o s y r m i i
e o r e o g n a k r t t m a h u l
w e m j e o e w o l f n k d a l l
p a a r d b z m p s l o i r i f a
p k a t r z t n e u s h o o r n r
```

Dutch	English
kangoeroe *[m]*	kangaroo
lynx *[m]*	lynx
neushoorn *[m]*	rhinoceros
jachtluipaard *[n]*	cheetah
olifant *[m]*	elephant
giraffe *[f]*	giraffe
varken *[n]*	pig
gorilla *[m]*	gorilla
das *[m]*	badger
luipaard *[n]*	leopard
stier *[m]*	bull
wolf *[m]*	wolf
lama *[m]*	llama
paard *[n]*	horse

Word Search #4 - Animals

s	i	t	a	r	g	a	o	r	b	f	k	p	s	w	g	r
i	s	l	b	p	j	z	a	m	u	h	a	e	m	s	i	o
p	h	x	n	y	l	e	d	o	r	r	d	b	r	t	r	t
s	o	v	c	c	p	a	a	x	b	e	n	y	l	i	a	a
t	k	a	n	g	o	e	r	o	e	x	a	l	d	n	f	g
z	v	e	j	b	w	m	u	w	v	e	p	c	c	k	f	i
r	o	e	x	n	t	i	k	z	u	m	m	w	h	d	e	l
k	g	d	r	a	a	p	k	h	s	e	y	m	v	i	k	l
n	h	n	r	o	o	h	s	u	e	n	e	n	g	e	g	a
j	d	a	p	c	o	t	n	f	l	e	l	l	v	r	i	w

Dutch	English
aap *[m]*	monkey
neushoorn *[m]*	rhinoceros
leeuw *[m]*	lion
rode lynx *[m]*	bobcat
kangoeroe *[m]*	kangaroo
stinkdier *[n]*	squirrel
alligator *[m]*	alligator
giraffe *[f]*	giraffe
vos *[m]*	fox
panda *[m]*	panda
rat *[m]*	rat
paard *[n]*	horse
pad *[m]*	toad
koe *[f]*	cow

6

Word Search #5 - Animals

```
e a r b e z b d o g m u r d i e r
f m a k o l a c i p a n d a c n w
a h m a b o n r g w m s r y e y m
y w a n g z a k e e k h o o r n n
s c r g f f z d r a a p g n s x s
a d h o f m v o x l a m t f n z t
d y f e k g c k a m e e l y d r c
i a a r d v a r k e n x l i y o e
o t e o o b c l e z e l i u m d e
d b r e p v k r o k o d i l j w t
```

Dutch	English
giraffe *[f]*	giraffe
aardvarken *[n]*	aardvark
krokodil *[m]*	crocodile
wangzakeekhoorn *[m]*	chipmunk
paard *[n]*	horse
dier *[n]*	animal
lynx *[m]*	lynx
zebra *[m]*	zebra
lam *[n]*	lamb
kangoeroe *[m]*	kangaroo
muilezel *[m]*	mule
panda *[m]*	panda
kameel *[m]*	camel
das *[m]*	badger

Word Search #6 - Around the House

```
n e g e e n n o m e t r o p f w s
d d n s u m z h e k s a t d n a h
v a e i z f b s m n r f d m z h p
h l u f b l v c h a z a w n b k g
d i u p r v s h t p w r a x o o m
d r i n k g l a s d z r e n v l i
v s p m a l k a z a m e s n l k k
l e t o h c s l u a j x z b v m f
c l c l e t e k z r l z w a c g c
m f l h r w t e k b c z t c e t k
```

Dutch	English
schaal *[m]*	plate
portemonnee *[m]*	purse
braadpan *[f]*	frying pan
handtas *[f]*	handbag
zaklamp *[f]*	torch
fles *[f]*	bottle
ketel *[m]*	kettle
vat *[n]*	pail
lade *[m]*	drawer
klok *[m]*	clock
drinkglas *[n]*	drinking glass
kraan *[m]*	tap
schotel *[m]*	dish
mes *[n]*	knife

Word Search #7 - Around the House

```
r m l m p j f v s t m h h n k z m
s t o a l e l r d f s g o m c j t
m s k k e v n e k a l a f v o r k
k a a t g w h x t c l n k r c a c
f k d z e i v t e l e v i s i e k
b e w s i e k a b s i n l i u v i
b d a z p o r t e m o n n e e b l
x a p f s f m a a r j f d v w s b
x l i h e j w a s m a c h i n e b
n b k n g z u u c r g o r d i j n
```

Dutch	English
gordijn *[n]*	curtain
kast *[m]*	cabinet
dak *[n]*	roof
raam *[n]*	window
portemonnee *[m]*	purse
vork *[m]*	fork
vuilnisbak *[m]*	rubbish can
wasmachine *[f]*	washing machine
blik *[n]*	tin
laken *[n]*	sheet
televisie *[f]*	television
ladekast *[m]*	dresser
spiegel *[m]*	mirror
kom *[m]*	bowl

Word Search #8 - Around the House

w	b	e	d	n	t	s	a	k	l	e	o	k	e	x	m	t
i	s	t	o	f	z	u	i	g	e	r	b	z	n	d	i	e
a	l	k	n	a	p	d	a	a	r	b	p	i	v	u	x	l
f	d	n	j	i	d	r	o	g	e	h	c	u	o	d	e	i
v	d	i	t	a	v	s	s	h	m	l	w	c	p	t	r	o
j	b	s	k	w	r	a	c	a	s	e	j	u	c	s	f	t
g	f	l	a	h	l	u	m	f	g	f	j	l	k	h	j	m
v	u	t	r	g	o	a	c	c	f	a	b	l	i	k	d	l
b	e	p	s	d	i	v	h	u	v	t	j	j	i	e	x	e
r	c	f	v	t	e	l	e	v	i	s	i	e	b	u	z	r

Dutch	English
douche *[m]*	shower
vat *[n]*	pail
douchegordijn *[n]*	shower curtain
water *[n]*	water
koelkast *[m]*	refrigerator
tafel *[f]*	table
braadpan *[f]*	frying pan
toilet *[n]*	toilet
blik *[n]*	tin
bed *[n]*	bed
glas *[n]*	glass
stofzuiger *[m]*	hoover
mixer *[m]*	mixer
televisie *[f]*	television

10

Word Search #9 - Around the House

```
h  l  l  g  l  j  s  g  k  l  x  j  m  s  w  b  b
f  e  u  f  k  o  b  o  d  z  h  a  i  a  u  b  v
p  h  j  e  o  k  e  u  e  z  x  t  x  a  j  s  t
n  c  b  d  d  l  n  v  u  i  t  s  e  v  l  p  v
o  a  z  e  k  o  c  a  r  t  x  a  r  u  j  i  f
n  k  c  a  d  z  k  o  l  k  f  k  r  x  k  e  g
n  v  s  f  h  f  z  g  o  p  g  o  n  a  a  g  p
w  t  i  o  i  d  a  r  h  a  f  b  t  h  m  e  x
d  i  e  p  v  r  i  e  z  e  r  x  m  h  b  l  j
r  h  b  a  p  t  e  l  e  v  i  s  i  e  a  g  t
```

Dutch	English
bed *[n]*	bed
mixer *[m]*	mixer
televisie *[f]*	television
plank *[m]*	shelf
klok *[m]*	clock
diepvriezer *[m]*	freezer
kast *[m]*	cabinet
spiegel *[m]*	mirror
doos *[m]*	box
kachel *[m]*	stove
vaas *[f]*	vase
deur *[m]*	door
koelkast *[m]*	refrigerator
radio *[m]*	radio

Word Search #10 - Around the House

```
z j h a p o h u i s f l e s f m t
o k l e e n n o m e t r o p o t k
r e z e i r v p e i d x a n x o d
k v u i l n i s b a k w o m e g d
c o a k a b s a r a s t o e l r n
b z l d h n p z r u u m b d c s m
v c r k x i p n z w j x m a b a v
h f l r j i n h z i f z k p d l k
w m a d p a r t b d g o h o r g n
k r i p a k e u k e n i c t i z i
```

Dutch	English
doos *[m]*	box
portemonnee *[m]*	wallet
trap *[f]*	staircase
keuken *[f]*	kitchen
muur *[m]*	wall
klok *[m]*	clock
vuilnisbak *[m]*	rubbish can
asbak *[m]*	ashtray
glas *[n]*	glass
pot *[m]*	pot
huis *[n]*	house
diepvriezer *[m]*	freezer
fles *[f]*	bottle
stoel *[m]*	chair

12

Word Search #11 - Clothing

```
n  t  t  r  u  i  k  z  o  z  u  g  s  r  n  o  n
z  v  l  i  n  d  e  r  d  a  s  t  v  t  l  u  i
o  n  d  e  r  b  r  o  e  k  g  s  y  t  o  k  l
b  d  s  k  o  u  s  e  n  p  h  h  n  m  k  b  n
y  k  o  r  s  e  t  m  o  n  a  i  h  m  b  e  i
r  l  g  z  u  y  p  n  t  s  n  r  d  a  s  h  i
p  s  e  t  t  o  o  r  g  t  j  t  a  l  a  a  c
i  n  i  k  i  b  g  j  z  m  y  a  n  p  j  m  k
n  e  n  e  o  h  c  s  l  e  d  n  a  w  l  p  a
n  r  l  k  v  c  f  w  i  i  t  g  m  l  a  u  p
```

Dutch	English
kousen *[mf]*	stockings
wandelschoenen *[m]*	hiking boots
beha *[m]*	bra
t-shirt *[n]*	T-shirt
korset *[n]*	corset
jas *[f]*	coat
trui *[m]*	jumper
vlinderdas *[m]*	bow tie
bikini *[m]*	bikini
pak *[n]*	suit
sjaal *[m]*	scarf
grootte *[f]*	size
onderbroek *[m]*	briefs
paraplu *[f]*	umbrella

Word Search #12 - Clothing

```
o k e o d k a z n e l a d n a s v
w p h t y t a h a n d s c h o e n
j k a p d a b b j h a d c d i b w
g s p o r t s c h o e n e n v v m
i j y g v e g i b e w l f h f h r
k s e g a h e b w d j y j z e h o
r s p i j k e r b r o e k b w n f
u z r d c b h t s p a k l p j f i
n u o v e r j a s v g s k f c m n
l s k e f s t r o p d a s t i r u
```

Dutch	English
rits *[m]*	zip
rok *[m]*	skirt
handschoen *[m]*	glove
spijkerbroek *[m]*	jeans
hoed *[m]*	hat
zakdoek *[m]*	handkerchief
overjas *[m]*	overcoat
pak *[n]*	suit
beha *[m]*	bra
badpak *[n]*	bathing suit
uniform *[n]*	jumpsuit
sandalen *[m]*	sandals
stropdas *[m]*	necktie
sportschoenen *[m]*	running shoes

Word Search #13 - Clothing

```
h a o u m o h h e m d g u b h f k
m o w a n d e l s c h o e n e n d
t f e u l r k e d m k h g o m j b
o l z d c a d a e f o l g g f n d
l y m u m j o i b k b n e i n z a
l l s v e a r h p f l i w r v s f
i h a n d s c h o e n e n v e l a
a b o f b k p a n t a l o n n n h
m y p e j p i l s d d p a k z r e
c u n e l a d n a s t s h i r t b
```

Dutch	English
pak *[n]*	suit
wandelschoenen *[m]*	hiking boots
handschoenen *[m]*	gloves
jas *[f]*	coat
hemd *[n]*	shirt
sandalen *[m]*	sandals
maillot *[m]*	tights
pantalon *[m]*	trousers
kleren *[f]*	clothes
t-shirt *[n]*	T-shirt
riem *[m]*	belt
beha *[m]*	bra
slipje *[n]*	knickers
hoed *[m]*	hat

Word Search #14 - Clothing

```
w  c  c  s  i  b  g  r  i  w  r  m  e  c  t  b  a
j  i  a  r  c  w  h  a  w  y  i  g  i  e  i  k  o
v  j  k  a  p  d  a  b  k  r  t  p  s  k  e  v  a
o  l  r  z  a  k  d  o  e  k  s  r  i  b  e  r  t
d  e  o  h  v  u  p  n  v  i  o  n  l  r  m  c  u
t  s  e  v  d  c  i  y  i  k  i  o  a  k  e  w  i
s  u  d  v  p  d  t  s  p  b  e  l  r  y  i  n  b
w  t  t  o  l  l  i  a  m  s  l  u  t  i  r  j  t
b  o  y  p  i  v  l  g  r  o  o  t  t  e  u  p  z
d  e  v  a  r  n  e  s  u  o  k  z  s  e  d  o  y
```

Dutch	English
hoed *[m]*	hat
riem *[m]*	belt
vest *[n]*	waistcoat
maillot *[m]*	tights
overall *[m]*	overalls
grootte *[f]*	size
bloes *[f]*	blouse
zakdoek *[m]*	handkerchief
bikini *[m]*	bikini
rits *[m]*	zip
jas *[f]*	coat
korset *[n]*	corset
badpak *[n]*	bathing suit
kousen *[mf]*	stockings

Word Search #15 - Clothing

```
r v s o n k e o r b r e d n o m r
e j z b v l i n d e r d a s l f s
l z s z s p i j k e r b r o e k r
f m k a p y z k a p d a b p g c e
y g r n e n e o h c s t r o p s p
s t r o p d a s a j d a b i z y p
p u z o f w v b i k i n i j e l i
y i m l g i j v e s m f f o f m l
l i t f i g n r l n e s u o k c s
g d u s l k v u t o l l i a m s t
```

Dutch	English
riem *[m]*	belt
sportschoenen *[m]*	running shoes
spijkerbroek *[m]*	jeans
stropdas *[m]*	necktie
uniform *[n]*	jumpsuit
badpak *[n]*	bathing suit
vlinderdas *[m]*	bow tie
slippers *[m]*	slippers
kousen *[mf]*	stockings
badjas *[f]*	dressing gown
maillot *[m]*	tights
bikini *[m]*	bikini
pak *[n]*	suit
onderbroek *[m]*	briefs

Word Search #16 - Colours

```
t  h  e  k  p  p  t  a  n  b  h  g  r  i  j  s  k
g  e  e  l  i  n  j  i  r  u  e  l  k  i  w  n  i
p  k  z  r  j  w  k  r  w  r  p  g  n  l  d  e  t
z  e  u  p  p  h  o  b  u  b  e  s  r  t  t  o  p
b  b  s  r  i  z  e  j  t  k  l  d  z  o  l  p  g
l  r  w  p  e  i  l  o  o  j  s  o  l  l  e  e  a
a  u  h  o  g  k  e  j  n  a  r  o  n  e  z  n  j
u  i  s  e  k  n  n  p  j  t  l  d  k  d  h  a  e
w  n  z  o  r  t  d  o  n  k  e  r  b  r  u  i  n
a  l  d  g  p  j  d  t  d  s  s  z  a  t  h  t  p
```

Dutch	English
blond *[adj]*	blond
wit *[adj]*	white
roze *[adj]*	pink
donkerbruin *[adj]*	maroon
bruin *[adj]*	brown
helder *[adj]*	bright
groen *[adj]*	green
kleur *[m]*	colour
grijs *[adj]*	grey
oranje *[adj]*	orange
blauw *[adj]*	blue
donker *[adj]*	dark
beige *[adj]*	beige
geel *[adj]*	yellow

Word Search #17 - Colours

```
h b g w u a l b a a e g r o e n o
s j p a u g j u z i r e k n o d g
d i t w e o s w g r u e l k n r z
i n i o o r a h i e s u j w i e l
d u r g a r z r j b n t o j t d e
n w s a t u w n k p b i s e r l e
s d p g j r a u o r k k s r d e g
n g w z t r o g u h i k k s b h r
r n b i o p j i s k g d o o r e z
k u w d d o n k e r b r u i n b w
```

Dutch	English
grijs *[adj]*	grey
kleur *[m]*	colour
bruin *[adj]*	brown
zwart *[adj]*	black
helder *[adj]*	bright
rood *[adj]*	red
wit *[adj]*	white
oranje *[adj]*	orange
geel *[adj]*	yellow
blauw *[adj]*	blue
paars *[adj]*	purple
donkerbruin *[adj]*	maroon
donker *[adj]*	dark
groen *[adj]*	green

Word Search #18 - Colours

```
z e g i e b i b s k l e u r z w p
i t b j g d l o b g d u g e e l n
g p t r l a b r u i n e a s i g n
g n o e u g z e j n a r o g j k h
a e d w t s u i t i w r s h e d z
n j o g k n b t h d p a a r s r z
p s n d o n k e r b r u i n n i k
e z o r g g l b b a r r e d l e h
k t g s k d a g u h w d o n k e r
j i t p g i t n d d w z t r e s p
```

Dutch	English
bruin *[adj]*	brown
paars *[adj]*	purple
wit *[adj]*	white
blauw *[adj]*	blue
zwart *[adj]*	black
kleur *[m]*	colour
groen *[adj]*	green
roze *[adj]*	pink
donkerbruin *[adj]*	maroon
beige *[adj]*	beige
helder *[adj]*	bright
oranje *[adj]*	orange
donker *[adj]*	dark
geel *[adj]*	yellow

Word Search #19 - Colours

```
d t a e w u n z n b e h w s i w l
i n g i g t i e s n r j e s s u i
r p t s b i d e o k a u k u j a n
h s j g l b e s b r d g i h i l z
n h i b o j u b u h g o r n r b s
o t w n n s k l e u r u o r g o w
l k e a d d o n k e r i b r e r e
h k r j h e l d e r e a k i o p z
d o n k e r b r u i n h n b e z t
s z n g w b p r z u w o z s w w e
```

Dutch	English
oranje *[adj]*	orange
groen *[adj]*	green
wit *[adj]*	white
bruin *[adj]*	brown
helder *[adj]*	bright
blauw *[adj]*	blue
donkerbruin *[adj]*	maroon
blond *[adj]*	blond
donker *[adj]*	dark
beige *[adj]*	beige
roze *[adj]*	pink
rood *[adj]*	red
kleur *[m]*	colour
grijs *[adj]*	grey

Word Search #20 - Colours

```
d a r n j r t t w l n g a z o j z
j g n d s d r e d o n k e r g l g
t k u o g t a j n s i t g i e b r
e b l o k h w n t r p h d p e l i
e z g r a e z a j a t l b d l o j
o i i w n l e r i a r o z e h n s
b d o k j d g o u p w w p p e d n
j h t b d e a r n n r i z u k d u
r u e l k r i w u a l b t b k a n
r u j r b n d o n k e r b r u i n
```

Dutch	English
zwart *[adj]*	black
helder *[adj]*	bright
rood *[adj]*	red
roze *[adj]*	pink
paars *[adj]*	purple
donkerbruin *[adj]*	maroon
blauw *[adj]*	blue
blond *[adj]*	blond
oranje *[adj]*	orange
kleur *[m]*	colour
wit *[adj]*	white
geel *[adj]*	yellow
donker *[adj]*	dark
grijs *[adj]*	grey

Word Search #21 - Days, Months, Seasons

```
k w g d z r e b m e t p e s t g u
z k w e e d f g u t s f r e h a m
u z c o r c o o a g i t s f n d u
d b o n h s e n l d a w g t v s t
u r a n r w l m d b n d n c o n r
b v z s d w i j b e c a s m c i a
m t d h m a a n d e r j a n w d a
w l v l h f g v t e r d u m e r m
l u v s g a d c k e g s a l f o j
j z n u e t n e l k r k h g i l w
```

Dutch	English
winter *[m]*	winter
herfst *[m]*	autumn
december *[m]*	December
donderdag *[m]*	Thursday
zondag *[m]*	Sunday
lente *[f]*	spring
maand *[f]*	month
maart *[m]*	March
dinsdag *[m]*	Tuesday
september *[m]*	September
maandag *[m]*	Monday
juli *[m]*	July
dag *[m]*	day
woensdag *[m]*	Wednesday

Word Search #22 - Days, Months, Seasons

```
c  j  j  w  n  o  f  z  o  k  t  o  b  e  r  o  p
g  r  g  u  k  j  i  p  l  g  h  s  v  b  s  w  i
a  e  a  z  l  d  n  l  p  k  k  g  z  u  k  i  r
d  m  d  a  o  i  g  o  d  f  a  f  t  l  o  n  a
r  o  j  h  i  k  j  n  z  d  n  s  i  e  v  t  u
e  z  i  t  k  p  a  n  s  i  u  c  i  n  b  e  r
d  h  r  n  k  a  k  n  d  g  e  m  l  t  j  r  b
n  p  v  u  m  u  e  l  u  h  k  s  o  e  w  g  e
o  u  a  w  c  o  j  a  v  s  d  a  g  f  z  v  f
d  e  k  k  w  g  n  o  v  e  m  b  e  r  o  i  v
```

Dutch	English
zomer *[m]*	summer
dag *[m]*	day
seizon *[n]*	season
lente *[f]*	spring
augustus *[m]*	August
woensdag *[m]*	Wednesday
februari *[m]*	February
oktober *[m]*	October
november *[m]*	November
winter *[m]*	winter
juli *[m]*	July
donderdag *[m]*	Thursday
vrijdag *[m]*	Friday
maand *[f]*	month

Word Search #23 - Days, Months, Seasons

```
g  j  i  l  u  j  i  i  r  a  u  n  a  j  m  j  c
h  z  a  t  e  r  d  a  g  r  s  e  i  t  s  e  n
r  k  g  a  d  j  i  r  v  e  g  e  d  k  d  u  u
e  m  i  p  w  w  l  r  p  a  u  g  u  s  t  u  s
t  a  n  t  l  e  j  t  t  o  z  d  z  e  m  z  s
n  a  u  h  h  r  e  b  m  e  c  e  d  e  v  n  s
i  r  j  u  p  m  o  a  b  a  d  i  i  v  i  g  p
w  t  h  n  b  l  h  b  a  n  o  z  i  e  s  i  l
j  d  t  e  l  p  v  d  o  n  d  e  r  d  a  g  w
r  z  r  c  d  l  k  r  g  a  d  s  n  e  o  w  i
```

Dutch	English
mei *[m]*	May
september *[m]*	September
januari *[m]*	January
december *[m]*	December
zaterdag *[m]*	Saturday
augustus *[m]*	August
donderdag *[m]*	Thursday
juni *[m]*	June
vrijdag *[m]*	Friday
seizon *[n]*	season
maart *[m]*	March
juli *[m]*	July
woensdag *[m]*	Wednesday
winter *[m]*	winter

Word Search #24 - Days, Months, Seasons

```
d s n u a z a a r g a d n a a m c
m e o v r i j d a g s m a a r t w
z p v j u l i g n o z i e s h n o
b t e g i d m a t g f e b n e n e
s e m a z n j d l l j d k a r w n
e m b d l s t n r u e e w t f k s
j b e a t e k o p f l l s t s c d
p e r h g g p z f k i e m u t i a
b r i r a u n a j c g m j v g p g
d m l z g o d e c e m b e r v i w
```

Dutch	English
zondag *[m]*	Sunday
januari *[m]*	January
seizon *[n]*	season
maart *[m]*	March
herfst *[m]*	autumn
dag *[m]*	day
juli *[m]*	July
vrijdag *[m]*	Friday
maandag *[m]*	Monday
mei *[m]*	May
december *[m]*	December
september *[m]*	September
november *[m]*	November
woensdag *[m]*	Wednesday

Word Search #25 - Days, Months, Seasons

```
m i r a u r b e f v r i j d a g v
p w g a d r e t a z o s j f u f v
a j t g i z r e b o t k o s g e k
n z r e t n e l e g e h s f f e c
p n o w s g z t i e m c f j u l i
s c l m b t z e g a d s n i d v b
b s i v e e r e b m e t p e s a n
t r a a m r f h s g a d n a a m d
m n u z a e m e s p n o z i e s z
n b j v e o p a j u n i z w s l z
```

Dutch	English
juli *[m]*	July
lente *[f]*	spring
zomer *[m]*	summer
mei *[m]*	May
dinsdag *[m]*	Tuesday
zaterdag *[m]*	Saturday
vrijdag *[m]*	Friday
maart *[m]*	March
seizon *[n]*	season
september *[m]*	September
maandag *[m]*	Monday
juni *[m]*	June
februari *[m]*	February
oktober *[m]*	October

Word Search #26 - Family

```
r  d  k  z  z  u  s  t  i  e  f  v  a  d  e  r  e
e  g  t  c  g  s  k  t  b  e  u  v  t  m  z  k  o
d  k  c  a  r  z  h  o  d  n  i  k  n  i  e  l  k
a  p  p  e  o  c  z  l  e  i  l  i  m  a  f  d  h
v  w  d  l  i  z  m  n  e  t  n  a  w  r  e  v  a
t  u  e  n  s  l  v  p  d  n  n  e  e  f  e  l  o
o  w  z  t  h  d  s  t  i  e  f  m  o  e  d  e  r
o  r  z  c  n  n  o  o  z  f  e  i  t  s  w  t  g
r  u  d  m  b  a  w  r  e  t  h  c  o  d  k  b  k
g  h  g  r  o  o  t  m  o  e  d  e  r  z  k  l  u
```

Dutch	English
familie *[f]*	family
dochter *[f]*	daughter
nicht *[f]*	niece
stiefvader *[m]*	stepfather
grootmoeder *[f]*	grandmother
grootvader *[m]*	grandfather
pa *[m]*	dad
verwanten *[m]*	relatives
stiefmoeder *[f]*	stepmother
ouder *[f]*	parent
stiefzoon *[m]*	stepson
kleinkind *[n]*	grandchild
tante *[f]*	aunt
neef *[m]*	cousin

Word Search #27 - Family

```
c z s u f i h f b m m r d r s e d
f f t e n r p p p o e f i v t c o
o f e m o e d e r m i i u k i h c
a n l r o r d l r a m w r m e t h
b b z e z e w o c m r z b d f g t
g a m d p o p o k p n k k l z e e
d e n u m r d m r a o u a s u n r
l d i o f b f a m i l i e c s o m
u v n e t n a w r e v z i k t t o
e b u z i f z o v z u s b z g e f
```

Dutch	English
ma *[f]*	mum
familie *[f]*	family
moeder *[f]*	mother
zus *[f]*	sister
oom *[m]*	uncle
verwante *[m]*	relative
bruid *[f]*	bride
echtgenote *[f]*	wife
neef *[m]*	cousin
ouder *[f]*	parent
stiefzus *[f]*	stepsister
dochter *[f]*	daughter
zoon *[m]*	son
broer *[m]*	brother

Word Search #28 - Family

```
m m o z m h m c w s s e k u e n b
s a o p n f s t i e f m o e d e r
w e m t b h e f m o e d e r d t a
d t k z p i w b z p s n e e f n v
u n w a l p o i r e t h c o d a f
z a v i e t n a w r e v s t d w b
n t m t n w w g c w k i n e n r v
g a e t o n e g t h c e r h w e w
f t i t o o n e g t h c e p o v z
l d n g o l m n a m f n d l v m h
```

Dutch	English
verwante *[m]*	relative
echtgenoot *[m]*	husband
echtgenote *[f]*	wife
neef *[m]*	cousin
vader *[m]*	father
moeder *[f]*	mother
ma *[f]*	mum
stiefmoeder *[f]*	stepmother
familie *[f]*	family
tante *[f]*	aunt
verwanten *[m]*	relatives
dochter *[f]*	daughter
oom *[m]*	uncle
pa *[m]*	dad

Word Search #29 - Family

```
b t v a n o o z n s z t n e e f m
w h e i g r o o t m o e d e r t o
o c r z h p d i d c l a d l s u e
i i w a r e d e o m f e i t s w d
e n a a u r e o r b s v h e i p e
d a n v l n r e d a v f e i t s r
i o t n t e e c h t g e n o o t d
u i e g v u m o u h k n f d m z c
r g n e t n a w r e v i e w n a m
b r e t h c o d f e i t s g b r d
```

Dutch	English
stiefvader *[m]*	stepfather
bruid *[f]*	bride
verwante *[m]*	relative
stiefmoeder *[f]*	stepmother
broer *[m]*	brother
grootmoeder *[f]*	grandmother
zoon *[m]*	son
ma *[f]*	mum
stiefdochter *[f]*	stepdaughter
verwanten *[m]*	relatives
nicht *[f]*	niece
moeder *[f]*	mother
echtgenoot *[m]*	husband
neef *[m]*	nephew

Word Search #30 - Family

```
s  t  h  c  i  n  b  r  e  d  a  v  f  e  i  t  s
s  k  b  i  s  t  i  e  f  b  r  o  e  r  z  f  k
f  m  f  w  c  r  v  m  n  s  o  k  h  v  d  m  t
s  t  i  e  f  z  u  s  e  s  u  l  n  c  s  e  t
r  b  o  o  m  d  o  m  e  n  b  z  o  a  e  e  b
u  b  m  r  w  v  h  u  f  v  a  d  e  r  d  k  c
n  l  m  o  e  d  e  r  d  n  l  k  b  p  a  a  d
b  f  a  l  b  t  g  e  z  e  h  s  e  m  v  r  t
b  w  m  s  r  e  d  u  o  t  r  b  w  r  o  p  u
s  m  m  n  o  o  z  f  e  i  t  s  k  k  s  z  t
```

Dutch	English
ma *[f]*	mum
zus *[f]*	sister
vader *[m]*	father
neef *[m]*	nephew
moeder *[f]*	mother
stiefzus *[f]*	stepsister
ouder *[f]*	parent
oom *[m]*	uncle
stiefzoon *[m]*	stepson
stiefbroer *[m]*	stepbrother
ouders *[f]*	parents
stiefvader *[m]*	stepfather
nicht *[f]*	niece
pa *[m]*	dad

32

Word Search #31 - Numbers

```
l e z g i t f j i v s d w f f t z
l c d r i e h o n d e r d d n c d
n v e e r t i g g s w d o r e i v
e t o e u w w t o g e t n i g m g
i n l v f l o c z v w z g e u i i
t f d r e d n o h t h c a s t g t
r n e i t r e d h f e f r n z n r
e f i j w u v c d d n e i r s e e
e r o n z c a e j n m w w v s m d
v v a w n l i u j z t l l t e n u
```

Dutch

vier *[num]*

achthonderd *[num]*

dertien *[num]*

drie *[num]*

twintig *[num]*

acht *[num]*

veertien *[num]*

vijftig *[num]*

elf *[num]*

driehonderd *[num]*

zes *[num]*

twee *[num]*

dertig *[num]*

veertig *[num]*

English

four

eight hundred

thirteen

three

twenty

eight

fourteen

fifty

eleven

three hundred

six

two

thirty

forty

Word Search #32 - Numbers

```
n r f z e f e v d v e e r t i g n
e t o r h d r e d n o h h f l e s
i z r d r e d n o h n e v e z t f
t s j w t w d z a e z j e z u a s
t n e g e n t i e n e l l n e c r
h f r e e l o m u r s n a z w h s
c l c z i t e l e d t u c g i t z
a f i s w r g r i z i v h f v i a
f u f e t s d j h s g e t g c g o
d n e i t r e d s n o m u w e e s
```

Dutch	English
zestig *[num]*	sixty
honderd *[num]*	one hundred
twee *[num]*	two
elf *[num]*	eleven
negentien *[num]*	nineteen
achttien *[num]*	eighteen
een *[num]*	one
duizend *[num]*	one thousand
veertig *[num]*	forty
drie *[num]*	three
tachtig *[num]*	eighty
zevenhonderd *[num]*	seven hundred
dertien *[num]*	thirteen
acht *[num]*	eight

Word Search #33 - Numbers

```
a  n  n  v  i  j  f  t  i  e  n  w  s  t  u  z  n
a  i  e  z  e  v  e  n  h  o  n  d  e  r  d  e  h
n  j  o  e  u  n  a  c  h  t  h  o  n  d  e  r  d
t  z  z  l  z  l  e  z  l  v  v  g  o  u  z  e  c
a  w  v  w  v  z  h  o  i  i  c  r  e  g  r  h  j
l  g  i  t  r  e  e  v  j  t  h  v  r  t  o  i  g
s  w  l  r  f  z  c  f  s  l  r  g  i  t  s  e  z
v  t  w  a  a  l  f  c  g  i  i  g  r  c  u  s  v
c  z  e  s  t  i  e  n  m  n  l  m  r  m  l  m  i
u  d  v  e  e  r  t  i  e  n  g  a  t  a  a  d  t
```

Dutch	English
vijf *[num]*	five
veertien *[num]*	fourteen
miljoen *[num]*	one million
veertig *[num]*	forty
een *[num]*	one
aantal *[n]*	number
zevenhonderd *[num]*	seven hundred
achthonderd *[num]*	eight hundred
twaalf *[num]*	twelve
dertig *[num]*	thirty
vijftien *[num]*	fifteen
zestig *[num]*	sixty
zestien *[num]*	sixteen
elf *[num]*	eleven

Word Search #34 - Numbers

```
r g a r a t s n j r w e s v j d n
f i z f g i d e t n u l v n h w e
l t z t t e d i a t r g n s r n i
a r l c a n n t c z o m e u e h t
a e f l e n m f h j e l i e a c n
w e i z e e r j t j e m t e l f e
t v i u u w c i i e w m r r m e v
a u n m c u z v g s t r e h n t e
d r e d n o h n e g e n e l j z z
g u l i h o n d e r d u v g v u e
```

Dutch	English
negenhonderd *[num]*	nine hundred
een *[num]*	one
veertien *[num]*	fourteen
nul *[num]*	zero
duizend *[num]*	one thousand
tien *[num]*	ten
tachtig *[num]*	eighty
zeventien *[num]*	seventeen
veertig *[num]*	forty
twee *[num]*	two
honderd *[num]*	one hundred
vijftien *[num]*	fifteen
elf *[num]*	eleven
twaalf *[num]*	twelve

Word Search #35 - Numbers

```
w  n  g  h  t  l  o  g  h  u  c  d  w  l  e  t  f
f  r  g  u  t  g  j  c  o  s  n  e  i  t  r  e  d
i  n  e  i  t  t  h  c  a  g  i  t  r  e  e  v  d
n  g  m  c  n  e  g  e  n  h  o  n  d  e  r  d  s
c  h  n  e  o  j  l  i  m  z  e  v  e  n  t  i  g
r  t  d  s  e  z  n  e  i  t  n  e  v  e  z  j  l
r  w  n  f  l  e  t  w  e  e  h  o  n  d  e  r  d
m  e  n  i  v  g  i  t  s  e  z  n  e  e  w  u  v
g  m  g  i  t  h  c  a  t  g  i  t  n  i  w  t  f
e  u  u  a  h  o  n  d  e  r  d  a  o  e  i  j  n
```

Dutch	English
tachtig *[num]*	eighty
elf *[num]*	eleven
negenhonderd *[num]*	nine hundred
miljoen *[num]*	one million
zeventien *[num]*	seventeen
veertig *[num]*	forty
honderd *[num]*	one hundred
tweehonderd *[num]*	two hundred
twintig *[num]*	twenty
zeventig *[num]*	seventy
zes *[num]*	six
achttien *[num]*	eighteen
dertien *[num]*	thirteen
zestig *[num]*	sixty

Word Search #36 - Parts of the Body

```
r u u m t z l r g l j r m k g h r
c d e e t a r u e t g u t z s j
g m i k a a k l p v i s o d n a h
m b m l h i g a z e z e r j c g m
t b l i n d e d a r m g e o r h p
b n r k l i e r v t n l h i b g u
s j l i a k u s p o l u r e d a a
s i n p m h b e t i r j c e u d c
d d l e k n e o a v f e o s l o p
n z i i s b v t v g h e u p l u z
```

Dutch	English
klier *[n]*	gland
taille *[n]*	waist
ader *[m]*	vein
haar *[n]*	hair
tong *[n]*	tongue
hand *[n]*	hand
blindedarm *[n]*	appendix
enkel *[m]*	ankle
borst *[n]*	breast
kaak *[f]*	jaw
heup *[f]*	hip
dij *[f]*	thigh
pols *[m]*	wrist
lever *[n]*	liver

Word Search #37 - Parts of the Body

```
j  k  l  l  i  g  a  s  f  w  t  h  s  m  i  z  m
l  a  o  g  r  d  f  o  o  h  m  t  l  m  f  n  l
c  m  o  z  i  n  e  t  c  r  p  e  e  t  w  e  u
o  v  r  i  s  s  z  p  b  z  m  o  d  e  r  d  k
p  w  k  c  p  o  l  s  j  p  r  v  d  u  g  n  l
t  h  c  i  r  w  e  g  e  e  m  b  g  r  u  a  j
v  d  e  m  o  j  f  e  i  i  r  h  j  l  a  t  p
u  u  c  p  p  o  s  n  t  w  a  l  m  a  l  a  g
k  i  h  e  b  i  g  f  e  u  a  k  g  k  e  n  b
w  m  d  m  f  f  n  j  i  r  z  d  b  h  k  m  l
```

Dutch	English
pees *[n]*	tendon
iris *[f]*	iris
duim *[m]*	thumb
rug *[n]*	back
pols *[m]*	wrist
voet *[m]*	foot
gewricht *[n]*	joint
arm *[m]*	arm
nek *[m]*	neck
baard *[m]*	beard
hoofd *[n]*	head
tanden *[mp]*	teeth
oog *[n]*	eye
nier *[n]*	kidney

Word Search #38 - Parts of the Body

```
n b a a r d k k l i e r w a n g t
v b i i u i t o v h n j c d o b r
p i i f i u z r b z k d z b k s e
t s i u v s k g a h e i f v p w d
m r f j t b i w c h l n u m o z u
o b n e r s z w g a a m u b j i o
n t e r e v e l f t u b s j d z h
d n r t t n b r v e u s k l c j c
f j j k u n c o w t b c r i d a s
p i l o m f w d s l r h j c g u r
```

Dutch	English
baard *[m]*	beard
lever *[n]*	liver
buik *[m]*	belly
schouder *[m]*	shoulder
maag *[n]*	stomach
lip *[n]*	lip
teen *[m]*	toe
vuist *[n]*	fist
rug *[n]*	back
mond *[m]*	mouth
wang *[f]*	cheek
hart *[n]*	heart
enkel *[m]*	ankle
klier *[n]*	gland

Word Search #39 - Parts of the Body

```
m b l i n d e d a r m l e k n e r
u r n w z i t v b z r m n n c k t
n r k k m z h f b j r g d v r u h
e a g b o t c o o i i u m b e g h
t a b b k v i t r d i v i i l d t
e e o u m s z m s m z d b r v a b
o p n n i k e i t c p u e h i r r
r a g z g k g e k a n t f l h f k
p i h k m c o k a a k o l b h w r
s p t e o v u f s m n e o j i o f
```

Dutch	English
borstkas *[f]*	thorax
gezicht *[n]*	face
enkel *[m]*	ankle
rib *[n]*	rib
heup *[f]*	hip
bot *[n]*	bone
kaak *[f]*	jaw
taille *[n]*	waist
duim *[m]*	thumb
blindedarm *[n]*	appendix
buik *[m]*	belly
sproeten *[mp]*	freckles
dij *[f]*	thigh
voet *[m]*	foot

Word Search #40 - Parts of the Body

```
r  b  i  t  a  j  h  d  z  s  a  k  t  s  r  o  b
w  e  l  l  i  a  t  g  d  z  u  n  p  t  c  v  s
o  h  z  t  u  i  d  i  u  l  v  o  e  t  e  n  f
o  n  e  i  o  n  b  a  e  r  k  n  o  k  k  e  l
i  s  g  t  i  n  p  n  h  a  w  o  w  v  o  v  v
k  u  r  k  g  r  g  n  h  h  e  r  s  e  n  e  n
a  m  c  v  v  l  r  e  d  a  g  a  l  s  o  i  r
p  u  o  t  h  c  i  z  e  g  p  o  l  s  s  u  i
i  i  s  n  t  h  c  w  n  l  f  j  c  g  w  o  b
i  e  n  z  d  v  l  e  g  a  n  r  e  g  n  i  v
```

Dutch	English
voeten *[mp]*	feet
rug *[n]*	back
mond *[m]*	mouth
knokkel *[m]*	knuckle
slagader *[m]*	artery
tong *[n]*	tongue
borstkas *[f]*	thorax
kin *[n]*	chin
vingernagel *[m]*	fingernail
rib *[n]*	rib
pols *[m]*	wrist
hersenen *[f]*	brain
gezicht *[n]*	face
taille *[n]*	waist

Welcome to the
Word Scramble section!

For each category, there are 5 puzzles, and each puzzle has 7 word scrambles.

You must rearrange the letters of each scramble to get the correct word.

There is a place under each scramble to write your answer.

Spaces and hyphens are in their proper places already.

Word Scramble #1 - Animals

1) u j r a a g

_____

2) a d l u p i r a

_____

3) t k e k e r e v l s a n

_____

4) k o i l k d r o

_____

5) e n r m i e r e t e

_____

6) r a e k v n

_____

7) m l a

_____

Word Scramble #2 - Animals

1) r e t a p n

_____

2) e n y a h

_____

3) p a d

_____

4) b r z e a

_____

5) n t f a o i l

_____

6) o n i k n j

_____

7) n n o z a k a w k e o e g h r

_____

Word Scramble #3 - Animals

1) k o a l a

_____

2) r s h n o e n o u

_____

3) a a m l

_____

4) e k i n r t s i d

_____

5) s d a

_____

6) e r b e

_____

7) g i t e

_____

Word Scramble #4 - Animals

1) i r k k e k

_____

2) l a n i a r p j d

_____

3) n v b i a a a

_____

4) a e h y n

_____

5) e f b l f u

_____

6) a e p r n t

_____

7) l x y n

_____

Word Scramble #5 - Animals

1) n g a k r e e o n o k h a w z

_____

2) p e n a r t

_____

3) p a s h a c

_____

4) l m a

_____

5) e m l e a k

_____

6) s u h o n o r e n

_____

7) n y h a e

_____

Word Scramble #6 - Around the House

1)   l e k e t

_____

2)   e e p z

_____

3)   s a v a

_____

4)   r k a a n

_____

5)   t f l e a e a l k n

_____

6)   d l a e

_____

7)   k k n e u e

_____

Word Scramble #7 - Around the House

1) k l p a a z m

_____

2) r u u m

_____

3) n l k e a

_____

4) a a s b k

_____

5) e g l e p s i

_____

6) n h a t w a m s i a v e c a

_____

7) p z e e

_____

Word Scramble #8 - Around the House

1) b d e e l

_____

2) l e t s o

_____

3) l c h a a a k r e s

_____

4) r b d a m a k e

_____

5) f k e a l l n a e t

_____

6) o t e l o f n e

_____

7) o o s d

_____

Word Scramble #9 - Around the House

1) s u s s e a p n k l a

_____

2) a k z

_____

3) v l u k a b n i s i

_____

4) l s a g

_____

5) g e u r z f s t i o

_____

6) s m e

_____

7) t d k l a e s a

_____

Word Scramble #10 - Around the House

1) e o e e r t n n p m o

_____

2) k k l o

_____

3) d b e

_____

4) t p o

_____

5) u r u m

_____

6) o u c e h d

_____

7) a s t h n d a

_____

Word Scramble #11 - Clothing

1) r t o o e g t

_____

2) r s t i

_____

3) p a k d a b

_____

4) s h e e n n c d n l o a w e

_____

5) d n s v r i a d e l

_____

6) l a l i t o m

_____

7) a s j

_____

Word Scramble #12 - Clothing

1) j s a

_____

2) r l p p i s e s

_____

3) u t r i

_____

4) u k r j

_____

5) e t s o r k

_____

6) s p e i l j

_____

7) t - i s t h r

_____

Word Scramble #13 - Clothing

1) o k r

_____

2) j s a

_____

3) o g t e r o t

_____

4) r v e j o s a

_____

5) m i r e

_____

6) s a h h c n e o d n

_____

7) r u k j

_____

Word Scramble #14 - Clothing

1) a k p

_____

2) n a l s d n e a

_____

3) u j k r

_____

4) i i b i n k

_____

5) s e k k o n

_____

6) d e o h

_____

7) e o k d z a k

_____

Word Scramble #15 - Clothing

1) s e v t

_____

2) r a d s s o t p

_____

3) b o e l s

_____

4) d a b p k a

_____

5) a j a l s

_____

6) v e o a s j r

_____

7) s i l e j p

_____

Word Scramble #16 - Colours

1) a l b w u

_____

2) i t w

_____

3) r u l k e

_____

4) n d k r o e

_____

5) o e r g n

_____

6) u b n i r

_____

7) o d r o

_____

Word Scramble #17 - Colours

1) o d o r

_____

2) l e e g

_____

3) r o a n e j

_____

4) u n i r b

_____

5) i s g r j

_____

6) z a t r w

_____

7) r u k e l

_____

Word Scramble #18 - Colours

1) b k r e n n o r i u d

_____

2) e z o r

_____

3) e b g i e

_____

4) o d b n l

_____

5) e r u l k

_____

6) o j a n e r

_____

7) e g l e

_____

Word Scramble #19 - Colours

1) e z r o

_____

2) w u b l a

_____

3) l g e e

_____

4) d n o b l

_____

5) j a o e r n

_____

6) i w t

_____

7) k d r o n n e b i u r

_____

Word Scramble #20 - Colours

1) o k n r e d

_____

2) o r z e

_____

3) n e g r o

_____

4) o r b e n d k i n u r

_____

5) n u i b r

_____

6) t i w

_____

7) i e e b g

_____

Word Scramble #21 - Days, Months, Seasons

1) d s o e w a n g

_____

2) b e e d c r e m

_____

3) a i a j n u r

_____

4) b r e i u f r a

_____

5) d d g a d n r o e

_____

6) m z r o e

_____

7) e o k r b o t

_____

Word Scramble #22 - Days, Months, Seasons

1) b e o r n e v m

_____

2) d m a n a

_____

3) e s t b e p r e m

_____

4) s n d g d i a

_____

5) r i l a p

_____

6) o z g d a n

_____

7) t a a r m

_____

Word Scramble #23 - Days, Months, Seasons

1) b e p e s e m t r

_____

2) n v e m r b o e

_____

3) r n j a a u i

_____

4) i j n u

_____

5) e m i

_____

6) n d m a a g a

_____

7) o n a z d g

_____

Word Scramble #24 - Days, Months, Seasons

1) a m n d a

_____

2) e z o r m

_____

3) r i a g v d j

_____

4) e e l n t

_____

5) a d g

_____

6) n s a o e d w g

_____

7) j u l i

_____

Word Scramble #25 - Days, Months, Seasons

1) s i d n a d g

_____

2) f s r t e h

_____

3) e e e r s t b p m

_____

4) d w a s n e o g

_____

5) a p l r i

_____

6) j i l u

_____

7) a z d t a g r e

_____

Word Scramble #26 - Family

1) c t h n i

_____

2) o n z o

_____

3) s r f e b r t o i e

_____

4) u r s e d o

_____

5) m r e o d e

_____

6) o c o n t e e h g t

_____

7) e n f e

_____

Word Scramble #27 - Family

1) k d e l i n i n k

_____

2) e t r o g d e o r o m

_____

3) o m o

_____

4) e r d u o

_____

5) z o o n

_____

6) t c h n i

_____

7) w e v r a t n e

_____

Word Scramble #28 - Family

1)

e d o r s u

_____

2)

h r e e s t c t d i o f

_____

3)

h t o c d r e

_____

4)

p a

_____

5)

d k i i n k n e l

_____

6)

u s z

_____

7)

r a e v d

_____

Word Scramble #29 - Family

1) t e n a t

_____

2) o z o n

_____

3) t f i u s e s z

_____

4) a p

_____

5) o r e u d

_____

6) a m

_____

7) l f a i m i e

_____

Word Scramble #30 - Family

1) m o o

_____

2) e n w e r t a v

_____

3) i i a m f e l

_____

4) i c t n h

_____

5) f e n e

_____

6) r i b r e t o e f s

_____

7) e e o t h g e n t c

_____

Word Scramble #31 - Numbers

1) v r e i

_____

2) e e i e v t r n

_____

3) e d t o e r e h n d w

_____

4) v t i i f j n e

_____

5) m r i j a l d

_____

6) a t a a l n

_____

7) e n i t g n n e e

_____

Word Scramble #32 - Numbers

1) j l i d a m r

_____

2) e n t e e v n i z

_____

3) f i g j i t v

_____

4) o j i l m n e

_____

5) r t e d c d o h h a n

_____

6) v j f i

_____

7) d r e o v d e h n n e z

_____

Word Scramble #33 - Numbers

1) e t i g z s

_____

2) h r n d c o e h a d t

_____

3) d r i e

_____

4) r a l d m i j

_____

5) n e e i z v n e t

_____

6) e e o h n t d e d r w

_____

7) e g g t n e n i

_____

77

Word Scramble #34 - Numbers

1) e e t v n i r e

_____

2) t w a f l a

_____

3) o n l e m j i

_____

4) e z g v e i t n

_____

5) s z e

_____

6) z e v n e

_____

7) i e v r

_____

Word Scramble #35 - Numbers

1) w i t i g n t

_____

2) d m a r i l j

_____

3) n a a t l a

_____

4) e d d i d r e h o r n

_____

5) c a i t t h g

_____

6) e t e i r g v

_____

7) e n e z v

_____

Word Scramble #36 - Parts of the Body

1) r s i e p

_____

2) u m d i

_____

3) u r g

_____

4) c h e z t g i

_____

5) e l d d b i m a n r

_____

6) e e n t

_____

7) o l e d b

_____

Word Scramble #37 - Parts of the Body

1) e e n l k

_____

2) s s a b o t r k

_____

3) d a a s l r e g

_____

4) n e o e t v

_____

5) u r g

_____

6) p l i

_____

7) r i s e p

_____

Word Scramble #38 - Parts of the Body

1) r a a b d

_____

2) g o d l o i

_____

3) r m p i e w

_____

4) k a a k

_____

5) e e e s h r n n

_____

6) r l k e i

_____

7) t e a d n n

_____

Word Scramble #39 - Parts of the Body

1) n d l a b r m d i e

_____

2) t e h z g c i

_____

3) h r t a

_____

4) d l i g o o

_____

5) s o l p

_____

6) s i i r

_____

7) e i n k

_____

Word Scramble #40 - Parts of the Body

1) g a n u t e a g r g r

_____

2) l o e l e o g b

_____

3) r d e a

_____

4) l n e e k

_____

5) r e n i

_____

6) e p t e o r n s

_____

7) m d r d e l n i a b

_____

Welcome to the
Word Quizzes section!

For each category, there are 5 quizzes, and each quiz has 10 questions.

You must choose the best match for the word given.

Word Quiz #1 - Animals

Choose the best English word to match the Dutch word.

1) stinkdier
a) koala
b) rat
c) squirrel
d) goat

2) kikker
a) squirrel
b) porcupine
c) elephant
d) frog

3) zebra
a) tortoise
b) lynx
c) zebra
d) gorilla

4) koe
a) rabbit
b) cow
c) bear
d) camel

5) stier
a) bull
b) llama
c) squirrel
d) fox

6) bever
a) camel
b) sheep
c) beaver
d) zebra

7) stekelvarken
a) porcupine
b) lion
c) armadillo
d) hippopotamus

8) krokodil
a) rabbit
b) llama
c) crocodile
d) panda

9) neushoorn
a) donkey
b) rhinoceros
c) snake
d) llama

10) aap
a) monkey
b) jaguar
c) gazelle
d) armadillo

Word Quiz #2 - Animals

Choose the best English word to match the Dutch word.

1) lam
   a) goat
   b) tortoise
   c) lamb
   d) elephant

2) lynx
   a) panther
   b) alligator
   c) lynx
   d) camel

3) zebra
   a) rat
   b) rhinoceros
   c) fox
   d) zebra

4) olifant
   a) dog
   b) elephant
   c) gorilla
   d) tiger

5) schaap
   a) sheep
   b) armadillo
   c) frog
   d) kangaroo

6) hond
   a) dog
   b) lamb
   c) chipmunk
   d) armadillo

7) jaguar
   a) snake
   b) fox
   c) jaguar
   d) zebra

8) paard
   a) anteater
   b) horse
   c) cheetah
   d) llama

9) stinkdier
   a) squirrel
   b) goat
   c) toad
   d) llama

10) kangoeroe
   a) tortoise
   b) lamb
   c) kangaroo
   d) goat

Word Quiz #3 - Animals

Choose the best English word to match the Dutch word.

1) baviaan
a) chipmunk
b) baboon
c) bear
d) cheetah

2) hond
a) dog
b) tortoise
c) aardvark
d) snake

3) koala
a) anteater
b) koala
c) tiger
d) elephant

4) konijn
a) donkey
b) rabbit
c) baboon
d) panther

5) wolf
a) llama
b) wolf
c) dog
d) sheep

6) muis
a) cow
b) goat
c) mouse
d) squirrel

7) kat
a) toad
b) lamb
c) llama
d) cat

8) miereneter
a) anteater
b) hyena
c) porcupine
d) jaguar

9) leeuw
a) llama
b) wolf
c) lion
d) armadillo

10) wangzakeekhoorn
a) chipmunk
b) sheep
c) wolf
d) leopard

Word Quiz #4 - Animals
Choose the best Dutch word to match the English word.

1) panther
a) panter
b) jachtluipaard
c) kameel
d) poema

2) llama
a) gordeldier
b) lama
c) buffel
d) wangzakeekhoorn

3) toad
a) kat
b) pad
c) varken
d) hond

4) elephant
a) dier
b) hert
c) aardvarken
d) olifant

5) hyena
a) jachtluipaard
b) hyena
c) bever
d) schaap

6) cow
a) luipaard
b) krokodil
c) koe
d) rat

7) armadillo
a) gordeldier
b) miereneter
c) varken
d) buffel

8) anteater
a) miereneter
b) kameel
c) stier
d) panter

9) horse
a) paard
b) kangoeroe
c) schildpad
d) lynx

10) aardvark
a) gazelle
b) aardvarken
c) varken
d) buffel

Word Quiz #5 - Animals

Choose the best Dutch word to match the English word.

1) rat
  a) jachtluipaard
  b) rat
  c) das
  d) vos

2) aardvark
  a) beer
  b) kangoeroe
  c) aardvarken
  d) baviaan

3) hyena
  a) koe
  b) kameel
  c) hyena
  d) panter

4) leopard
  a) stinkdier
  b) rode lynx
  c) luipaard
  d) beer

5) donkey
  a) kameel
  b) hert
  c) gorilla
  d) ezel

6) horse
  a) beer
  b) paard
  c) zebra
  d) aap

7) sheep
  a) schaap
  b) kikker
  c) lama
  d) ezel

8) crocodile
  a) muilezel
  b) gazelle
  c) krokodil
  d) jaguar

9) frog
  a) varken
  b) kikker
  c) jachtluipaard
  d) olifant

10) jaguar
  a) jaguar
  b) gorilla
  c) neushoorn
  d) koala

Word Quiz #6 - Around the House

Choose the best English word to match the Dutch word.

1) televisie
a) television
b) dresser
c) glass
d) pot

2) tafel
a) chair
b) dishwasher
c) table
d) fork

3) vuilniszak
a) rubbish bag
b) floor
c) staircase
d) sleeping bag

4) plafond
a) dresser
b) ceiling
c) image
d) toilet

5) wekker
a) window
b) alarm clock
c) mirror
d) rubbish can

6) portemonnee
a) freezer
b) frying pan
c) chair
d) purse

7) plaatje
a) switch
b) sheet
c) picture
d) kitchen

8) laken
a) broom
b) shelf
c) purse
d) sheet

9) schakelaar
a) switch
b) chair
c) pillow
d) bath (tub)

10) keuken
a) drawer
b) kitchen
c) bag
d) freezer

Word Quiz #7 - Around the House

Choose the best English word to match the Dutch word.

1) wasmachine
a) kitchen
b) washing machine
c) fork
d) spoon

2) diepvriezer
a) freezer
b) napkin
c) image
d) toilet

3) badkuip
a) bath (tub)
b) tap
c) purse
d) glass

4) dak
a) dish
b) roof
c) furniture
d) rubbish bag

5) kom
a) drinking glass
b) bag
c) couch
d) bowl

6) schaal
a) fork
b) plate
c) house
d) telephone

7) radio
a) radio
b) bookcase
c) curtain
d) bottle

8) sleutel
a) drawer
b) key
c) purse
d) bath (tub)

9) mixer
a) couch
b) mixer
c) staircase
d) picture

10) asbak
a) staircase
b) ashtray
c) glass
d) floor

Word Quiz #8 - Around the House
Choose the best English word to match the Dutch word.

1) glas
a) table
b) glass
c) stove
d) curtain

2) portemonnee
a) rubbish can
b) purse
c) water
d) sheet

3) badkuip
a) bath (tub)
b) drinking glass
c) wardrobe
d) lamp

4) zaklamp
a) chair
b) washing machine
c) torch
d) image

5) vaas
a) frying pan
b) vase
c) bookcase
d) painting

6) stofzuiger
a) hoover
b) knife
c) plate
d) pillow

7) plafond
a) pot
b) ceiling
c) couch
d) image

8) dak
a) pillow
b) switch
c) hoover
d) roof

9) kledingkast
a) rubbish can
b) telephone
c) wardrobe
d) bag

10) bed
a) bed
b) pillow
c) vase
d) hoover

Word Quiz #9 - Around the House

Choose the best Dutch word to match the English word.

1) purse
a) vaas
b) zeep
c) lade
d) portemonnee

2) dish
a) kledingkast
b) radio
c) kast
d) schotel

3) dishwasher
a) gordijn
b) koffiepot
c) vaatwasmachine
d) ladekast

4) painting
a) diepvriezer
b) schilderij
c) bezem
d) braadpan

5) bath (tub)
a) vork
b) huis
c) deken
d) badkuip

6) mixer
a) mixer
b) boekenkast
c) ketel
d) droger

7) toaster
a) portemonnee
b) broodrooster
c) kop
d) huis

8) handbag
a) handtas
b) zeep
c) mes
d) badkamer

9) image
a) douche
b) ketel
c) beeld
d) kachel

10) cabinet
a) douchegordijn
b) asbak
c) tafel
d) kast

Word Quiz #10 - Around the House

Choose the best Dutch word to match the English word.

1) table
   a) huis
   b) tafel
   c) wasmachine
   d) kast

2) mixer
   a) beeld
   b) spiegel
   c) badkamer
   d) mixer

3) spoon
   a) lade
   b) water
   c) lepel
   d) klok

4) shower
   a) beeld
   b) douche
   c) vaatwasmachine
   d) schilderij

5) chair
   a) deur
   b) handtas
   c) vaas
   d) stoel

6) ceiling
   a) plafond
   b) water
   c) boekenkast
   d) laken

7) ashtray
   a) douche
   b) asbak
   c) water
   d) kop

8) torch
   a) klok
   b) plaatje
   c) stoel
   d) zaklamp

9) frying pan
   a) portemonnee
   b) broodrooster
   c) braadpan
   d) slaapzak

10) drier
   a) zeep
   b) keuken
   c) dak
   d) droger

Word Quiz #11 - Clothing

Choose the best English word to match the Dutch word.

1) sportschoenen
   a) running shoes
   b) clothes
   c) jumper
   d) overcoat

2) pyjama
   a) running shoes
   b) pyjamas
   c) briefs
   d) suit

3) pak
   a) suit
   b) hiking boots
   c) cardigan
   d) trousers

4) spijkerbroek
   a) glove
   b) briefs
   c) size
   d) jeans

5) badpak
   a) knickers
   b) cap
   c) bathing suit
   d) jeans

6) wandelschoenen
   a) T-shirt
   b) shirt
   c) hiking boots
   d) jacket

7) onderbroek
   a) overcoat
   b) briefs
   c) belt
   d) T-shirt

8) korset
   a) corset
   b) overalls
   c) glove
   d) jumpsuit

9) vest
   a) cardigan
   b) stockings
   c) suit
   d) cap

10) paraplu
   a) umbrella
   b) jumpsuit
   c) cardigan
   d) pyjamas

Word Quiz #12 - Clothing

Choose the best English word to match the Dutch word.

1) grootte
a) pyjamas
b) jeans
c) scarf
d) size

2) hemd
a) shirt
b) dress
c) corset
d) knickers

3) sokken
a) jumpsuit
b) glove
c) socks
d) briefs

4) trui
a) running shoes
b) dress
c) jumper
d) belt

5) sjaal
a) gloves
b) clothes
c) scarf
d) jumpsuit

6) jurk
a) dress
b) hiking boots
c) stockings
d) hat

7) maillot
a) tights
b) jeans
c) cap
d) jacket

8) vlinderdas
a) socks
b) bow tie
c) pyjamas
d) dress

9) rits
a) pyjamas
b) tights
c) zip
d) size

10) pak
a) clothes
b) dressing gown
c) suit
d) gloves

Word Quiz #13 - Clothing

Choose the best English word to match the Dutch word.

1) kleren
   a) size
   b) bra
   c) scarf
   d) clothes

2) spijkerbroek
   a) overalls
   b) dress
   c) trousers
   d) jeans

3) bloes
   a) belt
   b) clothes
   c) briefs
   d) blouse

4) pyjama
   a) dressing gown
   b) pyjamas
   c) briefs
   d) hat

5) bikini
   a) handkerchief
   b) jacket
   c) pyjamas
   d) bikini

6) sokken
   a) shirt
   b) knickers
   c) pyjamas
   d) socks

7) sjaal
   a) scarf
   b) socks
   c) jacket
   d) skirt

8) uniform
   a) gloves
   b) bikini
   c) jumpsuit
   d) umbrella

9) badpak
   a) cap
   b) jeans
   c) bathing suit
   d) sweatshirt

10) wandelschoenen
   a) bikini
   b) knickers
   c) running shoes
   d) hiking boots

Word Quiz #14 - Clothing

Choose the best Dutch word to match the English word.

1) cap
- a) trui
- b) sokken
- c) jas
- d) pet

2) overalls
- a) overall
- b) vlinderdas
- c) kleren
- d) stropdas

3) sandals
- a) overall
- b) sandalen
- c) spijkerbroek
- d) bikini

4) coat
- a) jas
- b) sjaal
- c) sandalen
- d) kousen

5) trousers
- a) rok
- b) pantalon
- c) sandalen
- d) jurk

6) scarf
- a) sjaal
- b) maillot
- c) rok
- d) uniform

7) dressing gown
- a) sandalen
- b) handschoen
- c) badjas
- d) overjas

8) stockings
- a) trui
- b) maillot
- c) kousen
- d) rits

9) T-shirt
- a) badpak
- b) overall
- c) t-shirt
- d) sjaal

10) shirt
- a) trui
- b) hemd
- c) rits
- d) pantalon

Word Quiz #15 - Clothing

Choose the best Dutch word to match the English word.

1) overcoat
a) spijkerbroek
b) overjas
c) uniform
d) sandalen

2) corset
a) vest
b) korset
c) slipje
d) riem

3) slippers
a) slippers
b) korset
c) zakdoek
d) grootte

4) jeans
a) beha
b) jurk
c) spijkerbroek
d) rok

5) hiking boots
a) onderbroek
b) wandelschoenen
c) jas
d) sandalen

6) briefs
a) overall
b) beha
c) onderbroek
d) kleren

7) suit
a) pak
b) rok
c) overall
d) kousen

8) zip
a) sandalen
b) pantalon
c) paraplu
d) rits

9) dress
a) sandalen
b) overall
c) jurk
d) jas

10) handkerchief
a) zakdoek
b) badpak
c) trui
d) jas

Word Quiz #16 - Colours
Choose the best English word to match the Dutch word.

1) donker
  a) dark
  b) grey
  c) yellow
  d) red

2) roze
  a) green
  b) red
  c) pink
  d) grey

3) bruin
  a) pink
  b) brown
  c) red
  d) blond

4) paars
  a) purple
  b) red
  c) blond
  d) grey

5) blond
  a) white
  b) bright
  c) dark
  d) blond

6) beige
  a) blue
  b) yellow
  c) purple
  d) beige

7) kleur
  a) yellow
  b) orange
  c) black
  d) colour

8) groen
  a) maroon
  b) red
  c) colour
  d) green

9) helder
  a) pink
  b) colour
  c) bright
  d) blond

10) grijs
  a) grey
  b) dark
  c) white
  d) red

Word Quiz #17 - Colours
Choose the best English word to match the Dutch word.

1) beige
   a) dark
   b) blond
   c) maroon
   d) beige

2) grijs
   a) green
   b) yellow
   c) grey
   d) orange

3) bruin
   a) green
   b) yellow
   c) brown
   d) blond

4) donkerbruin
   a) pink
   b) green
   c) white
   d) maroon

5) groen
   a) green
   b) black
   c) red
   d) colour

6) wit
   a) beige
   b) blue
   c) bright
   d) white

7) geel
   a) blue
   b) bright
   c) yellow
   d) pink

8) blond
   a) brown
   b) blond
   c) green
   d) yellow

9) paars
   a) red
   b) black
   c) purple
   d) grey

10) donker
   a) blond
   b) pink
   c) dark
   d) black

Word Quiz #18 - Colours
Choose the best English word to match the Dutch word.

1) paars
a) beige
b) brown
c) black
d) purple

2) blond
a) brown
b) grey
c) blond
d) purple

3) groen
a) black
b) bright
c) brown
d) green

4) donkerbruin
a) brown
b) purple
c) maroon
d) green

5) grijs
a) grey
b) black
c) orange
d) yellow

6) zwart
a) red
b) blue
c) black
d) green

7) beige
a) orange
b) beige
c) green
d) black

8) donker
a) dark
b) bright
c) black
d) grey

9) oranje
a) orange
b) grey
c) black
d) red

10) bruin
a) brown
b) grey
c) maroon
d) dark

Word Quiz #19 - Colours

Choose the best Dutch word to match the English word.

1) maroon
a) paars
b) oranje
c) donkerbruin
d) groen

2) blond
a) blond
b) oranje
c) beige
d) geel

3) dark
a) groen
b) donker
c) blauw
d) zwart

4) white
a) groen
b) roze
c) rood
d) wit

5) orange
a) bruin
b) donkerbruin
c) oranje
d) wit

6) yellow
a) geel
b) donker
c) kleur
d) zwart

7) red
a) paars
b) geel
c) blond
d) rood

8) green
a) donkerbruin
b) blond
c) groen
d) helder

9) colour
a) blond
b) blauw
c) kleur
d) grijs

10) beige
a) donker
b) roze
c) beige
d) bruin

Word Quiz #20 - Colours
Choose the best Dutch word to match the English word.

1) dark
   a) grijs
   b) groen
   c) beige
   d) donker

2) blond
   a) blond
   b) beige
   c) kleur
   d) wit

3) colour
   a) donkerbruin
   b) kleur
   c) blauw
   d) helder

4) brown
   a) zwart
   b) bruin
   c) rood
   d) groen

5) red
   a) kleur
   b) bruin
   c) oranje
   d) rood

6) black
   a) geel
   b) beige
   c) zwart
   d) blauw

7) white
   a) beige
   b) donkerbruin
   c) wit
   d) grijs

8) yellow
   a) blond
   b) groen
   c) geel
   d) wit

9) grey
   a) grijs
   b) kleur
   c) wit
   d) roze

10) blue
   a) oranje
   b) blond
   c) bruin
   d) blauw

Word Quiz #21 - Days, Months, Seasons
Choose the best English word to match the Dutch word.

1) maandag
a) June
b) Monday
c) September
d) autumn

2) donderdag
a) January
b) Thursday
c) month
d) Saturday

3) augustus
a) March
b) season
c) August
d) Tuesday

4) vrijdag
a) Friday
b) September
c) summer
d) Thursday

5) zaterdag
a) April
b) March
c) Sunday
d) Saturday

6) zondag
a) season
b) Sunday
c) November
d) spring

7) zomer
a) August
b) July
c) Thursday
d) summer

8) herfst
a) December
b) August
c) autumn
d) season

9) winter
a) April
b) March
c) Friday
d) winter

10) dinsdag
a) winter
b) November
c) day
d) Tuesday

Word Quiz #22 - Days, Months, Seasons

Choose the best English word to match the Dutch word.

1) april
  a) April
  b) March
  c) month
  d) Monday

2) zomer
  a) summer
  b) August
  c) Saturday
  d) winter

3) winter
  a) February
  b) October
  c) winter
  d) Wednesday

4) december
  a) winter
  b) December
  c) March
  d) November

5) maart
  a) August
  b) December
  c) March
  d) November

6) lente
  a) Tuesday
  b) spring
  c) Monday
  d) January

7) januari
  a) August
  b) Monday
  c) December
  d) January

8) seizon
  a) July
  b) season
  c) November
  d) autumn

9) mei
  a) May
  b) September
  c) day
  d) June

10) juni
  a) Monday
  b) June
  c) September
  d) summer

Word Quiz #23 - Days, Months, Seasons

Choose the best English word to match the Dutch word.

1) maand
   a) Wednesday
   b) month
   c) February
   d) December

2) februari
   a) November
   b) spring
   c) July
   d) February

3) vrijdag
   a) December
   b) October
   c) Monday
   d) Friday

4) september
   a) September
   b) December
   c) February
   d) July

5) winter
   a) winter
   b) April
   c) Sunday
   d) Saturday

6) november
   a) April
   b) winter
   c) March
   d) November

7) donderdag
   a) Thursday
   b) Friday
   c) January
   d) winter

8) juni
   a) season
   b) December
   c) April
   d) June

9) oktober
   a) October
   b) summer
   c) December
   d) January

10) zaterdag
   a) Saturday
   b) winter
   c) Thursday
   d) month

Word Quiz #24 - Days, Months, Seasons

Choose the best Dutch word to match the English word.

1) April
a) maandag
b) maart
c) april
d) herfst

2) Tuesday
a) woensdag
b) juni
c) zomer
d) dinsdag

3) day
a) januari
b) dinsdag
c) augustus
d) dag

4) February
a) zaterdag
b) februari
c) lente
d) december

5) Wednesday
a) zomer
b) woensdag
c) april
d) zondag

6) January
a) mei
b) januari
c) lente
d) zondag

7) June
a) mei
b) vrijdag
c) juni
d) woensdag

8) March
a) woensdag
b) winter
c) maart
d) september

9) season
a) november
b) dag
c) winter
d) seizon

10) spring
a) mei
b) lente
c) seizon
d) dag

Word Quiz #25 - Days, Months, Seasons
Choose the best Dutch word to match the English word.

1) spring
 a) zomer
 b) vrijdag
 c) lente
 d) juni

2) month
 a) november
 b) maand
 c) september
 d) oktober

3) February
 a) april
 b) seizon
 c) zondag
 d) februari

4) Sunday
 a) zondag
 b) dag
 c) december
 d) september

5) November
 a) april
 b) herfst
 c) november
 d) winter

6) season
 a) winter
 b) seizon
 c) dinsdag
 d) donderdag

7) August
 a) maandag
 b) augustus
 c) donderdag
 d) woensdag

8) May
 a) mei
 b) januari
 c) maandag
 d) zomer

9) Wednesday
 a) augustus
 b) woensdag
 c) januari
 d) februari

10) winter
 a) maandag
 b) november
 c) winter
 d) juli

Word Quiz #26 - Family

Choose the best English word to match the Dutch word.

1) bruid
   a) daughter
   b) sister
   c) bride
   d) aunt

2) stiefzus
   a) parents
   b) stepsister
   c) parent
   d) wife

3) tante
   a) parent
   b) nephew
   c) stepbrother
   d) aunt

4) neef
   a) relatives
   b) cousin
   c) sister
   d) son

5) oom
   a) uncle
   b) daughter
   c) parent
   d) son

6) pa
   a) bride
   b) mother
   c) dad
   d) father

7) dochter
   a) cousin
   b) husband
   c) daughter
   d) dad

8) echtgenote
   a) daughter
   b) grandmother
   c) family
   d) wife

9) zus
   a) sister
   b) dad
   c) cousin
   d) husband

10) vader
   a) father
   b) mother
   c) wife
   d) mum

Word Quiz #27 - Family

Choose the best English word to match the Dutch word.

1) echtgenoot
 a) bride
 b) husband
 c) stepdaughter
 d) dad

2) grootvader
 a) nephew
 b) grandchild
 c) grandfather
 d) stepbrother

3) grootmoeder
 a) husband
 b) bride
 c) daughter
 d) grandmother

4) pa
 a) parent
 b) bride
 c) dad
 d) mother

5) ouders
 a) stepmother
 b) parents
 c) stepsister
 d) aunt

6) zoon
 a) cousin
 b) son
 c) stepsister
 d) brother

7) stiefzoon
 a) family
 b) son
 c) stepson
 d) grandmother

8) echtgenote
 a) wife
 b) daughter
 c) parent
 d) mother

9) broer
 a) brother
 b) son
 c) nephew
 d) bride

10) oom
 a) relatives
 b) cousin
 c) uncle
 d) mum

Word Quiz #28 - Family
Choose the best English word to match the Dutch word.

1) ouder
 a) parent
 b) brother
 c) wife
 d) dad

2) broer
 a) stepmother
 b) brother
 c) cousin
 d) stepdaughter

3) stiefdochter
 a) stepdaughter
 b) stepsister
 c) brother
 d) wife

4) zus
 a) grandchild
 b) sister
 c) father
 d) grandfather

5) neef
 a) niece
 b) son
 c) nephew
 d) relative

6) echtgenoot
 a) relatives
 b) cousin
 c) grandmother
 d) husband

7) moeder
 a) parents
 b) mother
 c) grandfather
 d) sister

8) tante
 a) aunt
 b) daughter
 c) mother
 d) grandchild

9) bruid
 a) stepbrother
 b) bride
 c) cousin
 d) daughter

10) grootvader
 a) grandfather
 b) parent
 c) stepdaughter
 d) sister

Word Quiz #29 - Family

Choose the best Dutch word to match the English word.

1) brother
   a) vader
   b) kleinkind
   c) stiefvader
   d) broer

2) niece
   a) zoon
   b) oom
   c) nicht
   d) verwanten

3) relative
   a) stiefzoon
   b) vader
   c) verwante
   d) stiefmoeder

4) mum
   a) ma
   b) stiefbroer
   c) familie
   d) zoon

5) son
   a) zoon
   b) oom
   c) stiefzus
   d) pa

6) sister
   a) pa
   b) ouders
   c) oom
   d) zus

7) stepsister
   a) kleinkind
   b) echtgenoot
   c) stiefzus
   d) broer

8) wife
   a) stiefzus
   b) echtgenote
   c) stiefbroer
   d) nicht

9) mother
   a) pa
   b) kleinkind
   c) moeder
   d) ouders

10) relatives
   a) nicht
   b) broer
   c) verwanten
   d) bruid

Word Quiz #30 - Family

Choose the best Dutch word to match the English word.

1) uncle
a) ma
b) vader
c) echtgenote
d) oom

2) cousin
a) stiefzoon
b) stiefdochter
c) neef
d) broer

3) sister
a) ouders
b) stiefdochter
c) zus
d) grootvader

4) niece
a) dochter
b) nicht
c) neef
d) stiefzoon

5) bride
a) stiefmoeder
b) stiefzoon
c) kleinkind
d) bruid

6) grandfather
a) verwanten
b) echtgenoot
c) dochter
d) grootvader

7) parent
a) ouder
b) ouders
c) zoon
d) grootvader

8) son
a) familie
b) zoon
c) oom
d) ma

9) nephew
a) stiefzoon
b) ma
c) neef
d) familie

10) daughter
a) nicht
b) stiefbroer
c) stiefzus
d) dochter

Word Quiz #31 - Numbers

Choose the best English word to match the Dutch word.

1) duizend
   a) eleven
   b) one thousand
   c) nineteen
   d) six

2) nul
   a) zero
   b) one billion
   c) one thousand
   d) sixteen

3) tien
   a) six hundred
   b) nine
   c) ten
   d) sixty

4) tweehonderd
   a) five hundred
   b) two hundred
   c) fifteen
   d) eleven

5) elf
   a) five hundred
   b) seven hundred
   c) one hundred
   d) eleven

6) acht
   a) nine hundred
   b) seventeen
   c) eight
   d) six hundred

7) zeshonderd
   a) six hundred
   b) nineteen
   c) three hundred
   d) forty

8) achttien
   a) eighteen
   b) eighty
   c) twelve
   d) sixty

9) zeven
   a) fourteen
   b) seven
   c) six hundred
   d) nineteen

10) aantal
   a) five
   b) number
   c) seventy
   d) twenty

Word Quiz #32 - Numbers

Choose the best English word to match the Dutch word.

1) twintig
a) nine hundred
b) eighty
c) one billion
d) twenty

2) zeventig
a) nine hundred
b) seventy
c) one thousand
d) six

3) aantal
a) number
b) five
c) sixteen
d) eighteen

4) vijftig
a) eighteen
b) nine hundred
c) fifty
d) one thousand

5) veertig
a) nine hundred
b) forty
c) seventeen
d) fifteen

6) driehonderd
a) one thousand
b) eighteen
c) eight hundred
d) three hundred

7) zevenhonderd
a) sixty
b) seven hundred
c) eighteen
d) thirteen

8) zeven
a) seventeen
b) one thousand
c) twenty
d) seven

9) drie
a) fifty
b) eighty
c) three
d) sixteen

10) negentien
a) number
b) nineteen
c) six hundred
d) eighteen

Word Quiz #33 - Numbers
Choose the best English word to match the Dutch word.

1) miljoen
a) zero
b) five
c) seventeen
d) one million

2) honderd
a) two
b) five
c) eighteen
d) one hundred

3) twee
a) fourteen
b) five hundred
c) one
d) two

4) zestig
a) fifteen
b) eighty
c) sixty
d) thirty

5) nul
a) zero
b) five
c) two hundred
d) one million

6) vijftien
a) eight
b) three hundred
c) fifteen
d) two

7) zeventien
a) one hundred
b) one thousand
c) eleven
d) seventeen

8) tachtig
a) eighty
b) six
c) three
d) one thousand

9) vier
a) seventeen
b) eighteen
c) four
d) thirteen

10) negentien
a) thirty
b) nineteen
c) one hundred
d) eighty

Word Quiz #34 - Numbers
Choose the best Dutch word to match the English word.

1) eighty
   a) tweehonderd
   b) duizend
   c) elf
   d) tachtig

2) fourteen
   a) zeventien
   b) een
   c) veertien
   d) zestig

3) six
   a) vijftien
   b) drie
   c) miljoen
   d) zes

4) thirty
   a) tachtig
   b) dertig
   c) nul
   d) zeshonderd

5) sixty
   a) zestig
   b) achttien
   c) vijftig
   d) twee

6) eight
   a) zeventig
   b) negen
   c) zeventien
   d) acht

7) ten
   a) dertien
   b) zevenhonderd
   c) tien
   d) driehonderd

8) eighteen
   a) achttien
   b) zeventig
   c) twee
   d) vierhonderd

9) four hundred
   a) vierhonderd
   b) elf
   c) vijfhonderd
   d) honderd

10) one thousand
   a) twintig
   b) duizend
   c) zeventig
   d) negenhonderd

Word Quiz #35 - Numbers

Choose the best Dutch word to match the English word.

1) six
   a) aantal
   b) dertien
   c) zes
   d) tweehonderd

2) one thousand
   a) zestien
   b) twee
   c) duizend
   d) een

3) eighteen
   a) dertig
   b) elf
   c) achttien
   d) zeventig

4) two hundred
   a) dertien
   b) honderd
   c) acht
   d) tweehonderd

5) one million
   a) miljoen
   b) zestig
   c) twaalf
   d) tweehonderd

6) five hundred
   a) tachtig
   b) nul
   c) miljoen
   d) vijfhonderd

7) seven hundred
   a) veertig
   b) zestig
   c) negentien
   d) zevenhonderd

8) forty
   a) veertig
   b) elf
   c) acht
   d) negenhonderd

9) nineteen
   a) negenhonderd
   b) tachtig
   c) dertig
   d) negentien

10) ten
   a) nul
   b) miljoen
   c) tien
   d) aantal

Word Quiz #36 - Parts of the Body

Choose the best English word to match the Dutch word.

1) rug
   a) knuckle
   b) freckles
   c) back
   d) eyelid

2) lichaam
   a) body
   b) foot
   c) eye
   d) iris

3) ruggengraat
   a) artery
   b) backbone
   c) blood
   d) rib

4) knie
   a) freckles
   b) brain
   c) fingernail
   d) knee

5) slagader
   a) muscle
   b) heart
   c) rib
   d) artery

6) ooglid
   a) leg
   b) eyelid
   c) tendon
   d) throat

7) maag
   a) thorax
   b) blood
   c) stomach
   d) moustache

8) taille
   a) fingernail
   b) waist
   c) thigh
   d) eyelash

9) pols
   a) gland
   b) head
   c) beard
   d) wrist

10) snor
   a) moustache
   b) fist
   c) thorax
   d) waist

Word Quiz #37 - Parts of the Body

Choose the best English word to match the Dutch word.

1) bloed
   a) blood
   b) lip
   c) iris
   d) wrist

2) tanden
   a) tendon
   b) iris
   c) teeth
   d) beard

3) vingernagel
   a) fingernail
   b) artery
   c) hip
   d) wrist

4) voeten
   a) forehead
   b) feet
   c) stomach
   d) teeth

5) lever
   a) finger
   b) belly
   c) liver
   d) rib

6) vinger
   a) thigh
   b) skin
   c) finger
   d) arm

7) oor
   a) gland
   b) foot
   c) ear
   d) bone

8) maag
   a) stomach
   b) bone
   c) bladder
   d) rib

9) blaas
   a) ankle
   b) fingernail
   c) bladder
   d) elbow

10) dij
   a) jaw
   b) cheek
   c) thigh
   d) iris

Word Quiz #38 - Parts of the Body
Choose the best English word to match the Dutch word.

1) haar
 a) lip
 b) hip
 c) hair
 d) tonsils

2) voet
 a) skin
 b) mouth
 c) stomach
 d) foot

3) iris
 a) beard
 b) iris
 c) neck
 d) knee

4) borst
 a) throat
 b) wrist
 c) knee
 d) breast

5) hersenen
 a) brain
 b) toe
 c) iris
 d) artery

6) mond
 a) artery
 b) knee
 c) vein
 d) mouth

7) slagader
 a) neck
 b) artery
 c) face
 d) thorax

8) been
 a) leg
 b) ear
 c) artery
 d) thigh

9) vinger
 a) toe
 b) iris
 c) forehead
 d) finger

10) hart
 a) beard
 b) backbone
 c) heart
 d) teeth

Word Quiz #39 - Parts of the Body

Choose the best Dutch word to match the English word.

1) throat
 a) slagader
 b) keel
 c) knokkel
 d) pols

2) bone
 a) knokkel
 b) duim
 c) amandelen
 d) bot

3) neck
 a) knokkel
 b) duim
 c) nek
 d) zenuw

4) belly
 a) wenkbrauw
 b) borst
 c) oor
 d) buik

5) thigh
 a) klier
 b) dij
 c) lever
 d) hoofd

6) eyelash
 a) blaas
 b) wimper
 c) voorhoofd
 d) snor

7) chin
 a) kin
 b) oor
 c) huid
 d) knokkel

8) tonsils
 a) voet
 b) pols
 c) vinger
 d) amandelen

9) ankle
 a) hart
 b) enkel
 c) lichaamsdelen
 d) schouder

10) hand
 a) hand
 b) blaas
 c) sproeten
 d) lichaam

Word Quiz #40 - Parts of the Body

Choose the best Dutch word to match the English word.

1) feet
   a) voeten
   b) sproeten
   c) keel
   d) rib

2) breast
   a) snor
   b) iris
   c) borstkas
   d) borst

3) leg
   a) neus
   b) vuist
   c) been
   d) hart

4) eyelid
   a) gezicht
   b) gewricht
   c) ooglid
   d) iris

5) vein
   a) taille
   b) haar
   c) baard
   d) ader

6) tongue
   a) slagader
   b) tong
   c) bloed
   d) voorhoofd

7) lip
   a) baard
   b) gezicht
   c) tanden
   d) lip

8) gland
   a) klier
   b) borstkas
   c) long
   d) zenuw

9) thigh
   a) iris
   b) dij
   c) enkel
   d) wang

10) fingernail
   a) zenuw
   b) vingernagel
   c) maag
   d) tand

Welcome to the
hints and solutions section!

Here you can find the solutions to the word search puzzles, hints and solutions for the word scrambles, and answers to the quizzes.

Word Search Solution #1

k	a	d	n	a	p	t	d	y	w	p	e	j	b	o	a	r
m	s	l	a	m	a	n	a	a	i	v	a	b	h	y	o	p
w	a	n	g	z	a	k	e	e	k	h	o	o	r	n	e	p
b	m	r	s	t	i	n	k	d	i	e	r	y	i	s	o	v
b	u	i	a	u	k	r	w	c	c	d	p	s	c	r	g	e
c	i	h	h	d	e	j	o	n	r	o	o	h	s	u	e	n
y	s	z	g	i	a	t	l	d	r	a	a	p	i	u	l	j
d	w	v	t	e	t	z	f	g	a	z	e	l	l	e	i	w
n	s	s	x	a	n	s	p	f	w	a	s	p	f	o	w	k
r	o	v	k	w	h	i	a	i	d	r	a	a	p	v	e	p

Word Search Solution #2

x	a	d	n	a	p	c	p	o	f	g	n	a	l	s	t	p
k	o	n	i	j	n	y	a	w	o	l	f	c	v	r	y	z
j	a	c	h	t	l	u	i	p	a	a	r	d	e	z	x	z
r	a	n	e	l	e	z	i	y	x	d	s	h	j	v	f	s
e	a	i	s	h	b	n	r	o	o	h	s	u	e	n	j	f
i	m	w	a	n	g	z	a	k	e	e	k	h	o	o	r	n
d	k	w	s	t	j	t	i	j	g	e	r	p	v	y	u	z
r	o	d	e	l	y	n	x	j	u	j	v	i	l	j	r	g
i	b	d	t	h	h	h	g	r	e	i	t	s	n	h	v	i
k	g	g	m	r	n	v	o	s	f	l	b	e	e	r	n	s

Word Search Solution #3

m	b	c	t	h	i	d	a	s	j	p	l	a	m	a	d	l
e	s	t	i	e	r	m	d	p	z	a	x	y	d	u	r	n
i	o	w	e	f	f	a	r	i	g	v	h	o	n	p	a	g
d	r	a	a	p	i	u	l	t	h	c	a	j	v	x	a	o
s	p	d	o	d	h	v	a	r	k	e	n	g	s	d	p	r
d	k	x	v	t	n	a	f	i	l	o	s	y	r	m	i	i
e	o	r	e	o	g	n	a	k	r	t	t	m	a	h	u	l
w	e	m	j	e	o	e	w	o	l	f	n	k	d	a	l	l
p	a	a	r	d	b	z	m	p	s	l	o	i	r	i	f	a
p	k	a	t	r	z	t	n	e	u	s	h	o	o	r	n	r

Word Search Solution #4

s	i	t	a	r	g	a	o	r	b	f	k	p	s	w	g	r
i	s	l	b	p	j	z	a	m	u	h	a	e	m	s	i	o
p	h	x	n	y	l	e	d	o	r	r	d	b	r	t	r	t
s	o	v	c	c	p	a	a	x	b	e	n	y	l	i	a	a
t	k	a	n	g	o	e	r	o	e	x	a	l	d	n	f	g
z	v	e	j	b	w	m	u	w	v	e	p	c	c	k	f	i
r	o	e	x	n	t	i	k	z	u	m	m	w	h	d	e	l
k	g	d	r	a	a	p	k	h	s	e	y	m	v	i	k	l
n	h	n	r	o	o	h	s	u	e	n	e	n	g	e	g	a
j	d	a	p	c	o	t	n	f	l	e	l	l	v	r	i	w

Word Search Solution #5

```
e a r b e z b d o g m u r d i e r
f m a k o l a c i p a n d a c n w
a h m a b o n r g w m s r y e y m
y w a n g z a k e e k h o o r n n
s c r g f f z d r a a p g n s x s
a d h o f m v o x l a m t f n z t
d y f e k g c k a m e e l y d r c
i a a r d v a r k e n x l i y o e
o t e o o b c l e z e l i u m d e
d b r e p v k r o k o d i l j w t
```

Word Search Solution #6

```
n e g e e n n o m e t r o p f w s
d d n s u m z h e k s a t d n a h
v a e i z f b s m n r f d m z h p
h l u f b l v c h a z a w n b k g
d i u p r v s h t p w r a x o o m
d r i n k g l a s d z r e n v l i
v s p m a l k a z a m e s n l k k
l e t o h c s l u a j x z b v m f
c l c l e t e k z r l z w a c g c
m f l h r w t e k b c z t c e t k
```

Word Search Solution #7

r m l m p j f v s t m h h n k z m
s t o a l e l r d f s g o m c j t
m s k k e v n e k a l a f v o r k
k a a t g w h x t c l n k r c a c
f k d z e i v t e l e v i s i e k
b e w s i e k a b s i n l i u v i
b d a z p o r t e m o n n e e b l
x a p f s f m a a r j f d v w s b
x l i h e j w a s m a c h i n e b
n b k n g z u u c r g o r d i j n

Word Search Solution #8

w b e d n t s a k l e o k e x m t
i s t o f z u i g e r b z n d i e
a l k n a p d a a r b p i v u x l
f d n j i d r o g e h c u o d e i
v d i t a v s s h m l w c p t r o
j b s k w r a c a s e j u c s f t
g f l a h l u m f g f j l k h j m
v u t r g o a c c f a b l i k d l
b e p s d i v h u v t j j i e x e
r c f v t e l e v i s i e b u z r

Word Search Solution #9

h	**l**	l	g	l	j	**s**	g	**k**	l	x	j	**m**	**s**	w	b	b
f	**e**	u	f	k	**o**	b	**o**	**d**	z	h	a	**i**	**a**	u	b	v
p	**h**	j	e	**o**	k	e	u	e	z	x	**t**	**x**	**a**	j	**s**	t
n	**c**	**b**	**d**	d	**l**	**n**	v	u	i	t	**s**	**e**	v	l	**p**	v
o	**a**	z	**e**	k	o	c	**a**	**r**	t	x	**a**	**r**	u	j	**i**	f
n	**k**	c	**a**	**d**	z	**k**	**o**	l	**k**	f	**k**	r	x	**k**	**e**	g
n	v	**s**	f	h	f	z	g	o	**p**	g	o	n	a	a	**g**	p
w	**t**	i	**o**	i	**d**	**a**	**r**	h	a	f	b	t	h	m	**e**	x
d	**i**	**e**	**p**	**v**	**r**	**i**	**e**	**z**	**e**	**r**	x	m	h	b	**l**	j
r	h	b	a	p	**t**	**e**	**l**	**e**	**v**	**i**	**s**	**i**	**e**	a	g	t

Word Search Solution #10

z	j	h	a	p	o	**h**	**u**	**i**	**s**	**f**	**l**	**e**	**s**	f	m	t
o	k	l	**e**	**e**	**n**	**n**	**o**	**m**	**e**	**t**	**r**	**o**	**p**	**o**	t	k
r	**e**	**z**	**e**	**i**	**r**	**v**	**p**	**e**	**i**	**d**	x	a	n	x	**o**	d
k	**v**	**u**	**i**	**l**	**n**	**i**	**s**	**b**	**a**	**k**	w	o	m	e	g	**d**
c	**o**	a	**k**	**a**	**b**	**s**	**a**	r	a	**s**	**t**	**o**	**e**	**l**	r	n
b	z	**l**	d	h	n	p	z	**r**	**u**	**u**	**m**	b	d	c	**s**	m
v	c	r	**k**	x	i	p	n	z	w	j	x	m	a	b	**a**	v
h	f	l	r	j	i	n	h	z	i	f	z	k	**p**	d	**l**	k
w	m	a	d	**p**	**a**	**r**	**t**	b	d	g	o	h	**o**	r	**g**	n
k	r	i	p	a	**k**	**e**	**u**	**k**	**e**	**n**	i	c	**t**	i	z	i

Word Search Solution #11

```
n  t  t  r  u  i  k  z  o  z  u  g  s  r  n  o  n
z  v  l  i  n  d  e  r  d  a  s  t  v  t  l  u  i
o  n  d  e  r  b  r  o  e  k  g  s  y  t  o  k  l
b  d  s  k  o  u  s  e  n  p  h  h  n  m  k  b  n
y  k  o  r  s  e  t  m  o  n  a  i  h  m  b  e  i
r  l  g  z  u  y  p  n  t  s  n  r  d  a  s  h  i
p  s  e  t  t  o  o  r  g  t  j  t  a  l  a  a  c
i  n  i  k  i  b  g  j  z  m  y  a  n  p  j  m  k
n  e  n  e  o  h  c  s  l  e  d  n  a  w  l  p  a
n  r  l  k  v  c  f  w  i  i  t  g  m  l  a  u  p
```

Word Search Solution #12

```
o  k  e  o  d  k  a  z  n  e  l  a  d  n  a  s  v
w  p  h  t  y  t  a  h  a  n  d  s  c  h  o  e  n
j  k  a  p  d  a  b  b  j  h  a  d  c  d  i  b  w
g  s  p  o  r  t  s  c  h  o  e  n  e  n  v  v  m
i  j  y  g  v  e  g  i  b  e  w  l  f  h  f  h  r
k  s  e  g  a  h  e  b  w  d  j  y  j  z  e  h  o
r  s  p  i  j  k  e  r  b  r  o  e  k  b  w  n  f
u  z  r  d  c  b  h  t  s  p  a  k  l  p  j  f  i
n  u  o  v  e  r  j  a  s  v  g  s  k  f  c  m  n
l  s  k  e  f  s  t  r  o  p  d  a  s  t  i  r  u
```

Word Search Solution #13

h	a	o	u	m	o	h	h	e	m	d	g	u	b	h	f	k
m	o	w	a	n	d	e	l	s	c	h	o	e	n	e	n	d
t	f	e	u	l	r	k	e	d	m	k	h	g	o	m	j	b
o	l	z	d	c	a	d	a	e	f	o	l	g	g	f	n	d
l	y	m	u	m	j	o	i	b	k	b	n	e	i	n	z	a
l	l	s	v	e	a	r	h	p	f	l	i	w	r	v	s	f
i	h	a	n	d	s	c	h	o	e	n	e	n	v	e	l	a
a	b	o	f	b	k	p	a	n	t	a	l	o	n	n	n	h
m	y	p	e	j	p	i	l	s	d	d	p	a	k	z	r	e
c	u	n	e	l	a	d	n	a	s	t	s	h	i	r	t	b

Word Search Solution #14

w	c	c	s	i	b	g	r	i	w	r	m	e	c	t	b	a
j	i	a	r	c	w	h	a	w	y	i	g	i	e	i	k	o
v	j	k	a	p	d	a	b	k	r	t	p	s	k	e	v	a
o	l	r	z	a	k	d	o	e	k	s	r	i	b	e	r	t
d	e	o	h	v	u	p	n	v	i	o	n	l	r	m	c	u
t	s	e	v	d	c	i	y	i	k	i	o	a	k	e	w	i
s	u	d	v	p	d	t	s	p	b	e	l	r	y	i	n	b
w	t	t	o	l	l	i	a	m	s	l	u	t	i	r	j	t
b	o	y	p	i	v	l	g	r	o	o	t	t	e	u	p	z
d	e	v	a	r	n	e	s	u	o	k	z	s	e	d	o	y

Word Search Solution #15

```
r v s o n k e o r b r e d n o m r
e j z b v l i n d e r d a s l f s
l z s z s p i j k e r b r o e k r
f m k a p y z k a p d a b p g c e
y g r n e n e o h c s t r o p s z p
s t r o p d a s a j d a b i z y p
p u z o f w v b i k i n i j e l i
y i m l g i j v e s m f f o f m l
l i t f i g n r l n e s u o k c s
g d u s l k v u t o l l i a m s t
```

Word Search Solution #16

```
t h e k p p t a n b h g r i j s k
g e e l i n j i r u e l k i w n i
p k z r j w k r w r p g n l d e t
z e u p p h o b u b e s r t t o p
b b s r i z e j t k l d z o l p g
l r w p e i l o o j s o l l e e a
a u h o g k e j n a r o n e z n j
u i s e k n n p j t l d k d h a e
w n z o r t d o n k e r b r u i n
a l d g p j d t d s s z a t h t p
```

Word Search Solution #17

```
h b g w u a l b a a e g r o e n o
s j p a u g j u z i r e k n o d g
d i t w e o s w g r u e l k n r z
i n i o o r a h i e s u j w i e l
d u r g a r z r j b n t o j t d e
n w s a t u w n k p b i s e r l e
s d p g j r a u o r k k s r d e g
n g w z t r o g u h i k k s b h r
r n b i o p j i s k g d o o r e z
k u w d d o n k e r b r u i n b w
```

Word Search Solution #18

```
z e g i e b i b s k l e u r z w p
i t b j g d l o b g d u g e e l n
g p t r l a b r u i n e a s i g n
g n o e u g z e j n a r o g j k h
a e d w t s u i t i w r s h e d z
n j o g k n b t h d p a a r s r z
p s n d o n k e r b r u i n n i k
e z o r g g l b b a r r e d l e h
k t g s k d a g u h w d o n k e r
j i t p g i t n d d w z t r e s p
```

Word Search Solution #19

```
d  t  a  e  w  u  n  z  n  b  e  h  w  s  i  w  l
i  n  g  i  g  t  i  e  s  n  r  j  e  s  s  u  i
r  p  t  s  b  i  d  e  o  k  a  u  k  u  j  a  n
h  s  j  g  l  b  e  s  b  r  d  g  i  h  i  l  z
n  h  i  b  o  j  u  b  u  h  g  o  r  n  r  b  s
o  t  w  n  n  s  k  l  e  u  r  u  o  r  g  o  w
l  k  e  a  d  d  o  n  k  e  r  i  b  r  e  r  e
h  k  r  j  h  e  l  d  e  r  e  a  k  i  o  p  z
d  o  n  k  e  r  b  r  u  i  n  h  n  b  e  z  t
s  z  n  g  w  b  p  r  z  u  w  o  z  s  w  w  e
```

Word Search Solution #20

```
d  a  r  n  j  r  t  t  w  l  n  g  a  z  o  j  z
j  g  n  d  s  d  r  e  d  o  n  k  e  r  g  l  g
t  k  u  o  g  t  a  j  n  s  i  t  g  i  e  b  r
e  b  l  o  k  h  w  n  t  r  p  h  d  p  e  l  i
e  z  g  r  a  e  z  a  j  a  t  l  b  d  l  o  j
o  i  i  w  n  l  e  r  i  a  r  o  z  e  h  n  s
b  d  o  k  j  d  g  o  u  p  w  w  p  p  e  d  n
j  h  t  b  d  e  a  r  n  n  r  i  z  u  k  d  u
r  u  e  l  k  r  i  w  u  a  l  b  t  b  k  a  n
r  u  j  r  b  n  d  o  n  k  e  r  b  r  u  i  n
```

Word Search Solution #21

k	w	g	d	z	r	e	b	m	e	t	p	e	s	t	g	u
z	k	w	e	e	d	f	g	u	t	s	f	r	e	h	a	m
u	z	c	o	r	c	o	o	a	g	i	t	s	f	n	d	u
d	b	o	n	h	s	e	n	l	d	a	w	g	t	v	s	t
u	r	a	n	r	w	l	m	d	b	n	d	n	c	o	n	r
b	v	z	s	d	w	i	j	b	e	c	a	s	m	c	i	a
m	t	d	h	m	a	a	n	d	e	r	j	a	n	w	d	a
w	l	v	l	h	f	g	v	t	e	r	d	u	m	e	r	m
l	u	v	s	g	a	d	c	k	e	g	s	a	l	f	o	j
j	z	n	u	e	t	n	e	l	k	r	k	h	g	i	l	w

Word Search Solution #22

c	j	j	w	n	o	f	z	o	k	t	o	b	e	r	o	p
g	r	g	u	k	j	i	p	l	g	h	s	v	b	s	w	i
a	e	a	z	l	d	n	l	p	k	k	g	z	u	k	i	r
d	m	d	a	o	i	g	o	d	f	a	t	l	o	n	a	
r	o	j	h	i	k	j	n	z	d	n	s	i	e	v	t	u
e	z	i	t	k	p	a	n	s	i	u	c	i	n	b	e	r
d	h	r	n	k	a	k	n	d	g	e	m	l	t	j	r	b
n	p	v	u	m	u	e	l	u	h	k	s	o	e	w	g	e
o	u	a	w	c	o	j	a	v	s	d	a	g	f	z	v	f
d	e	k	k	w	g	n	o	v	e	m	b	e	r	o	i	v

Word Search Solution #23

```
g  j  i  l  u  j  i  i  r  a  u  n  a  j  m  j  c
h  z  a  t  e  r  d  a  g  r  s  e  i  t  s  e  n
r  k  g  a  d  j  i  r  v  e  g  e  d  k  d  u  u
e  m  i  p  w  w  l  r  p  a  u  g  u  s  t  u  s
t  a  n  t  l  e  j  t  t  o  z  d  z  e  m  z  s
n  a  u  h  h  r  e  b  m  e  c  e  d  e  v  n  s
i  r  j  u  p  m  o  a  b  a  d  i  i  v  i  g  p
w  t  h  n  b  l  h  b  a  n  o  z  i  e  s  i  l
j  d  t  e  l  p  v  d  o  n  d  e  r  d  a  g  w
r  z  r  c  d  l  k  r  g  a  d  s  n  e  o  w  i
```

Word Search Solution #24

```
d  s  n  u  a  z  a  a  r  g  a  d  n  a  a  m  c
m  e  o  v  r  i  j  d  a  g  s  m  a  a  r  t  w
z  p  v  j  u  l  i  g  n  o  z  i  e  s  h  n  o
b  t  e  g  i  d  m  a  t  g  f  e  b  n  e  n  e
s  e  m  a  z  n  j  d  l  l  j  d  k  a  r  w  n
e  m  b  d  l  s  t  n  r  u  e  e  w  t  f  k  s
j  b  e  a  t  e  k  o  p  f  l  l  s  t  s  c  d
p  e  r  h  g  g  p  z  f  k  i  e  m  u  t  i  a
b  r  i  r  a  u  n  a  j  c  g  m  j  v  g  p  g
d  m  l  z  g  o  d  e  c  e  m  b  e  r  v  i  w
```

140

Word Search Solution #25

```
m  i  r  a  u  r  b  e  f  v  r  i  j  d  a  g  v
p  w  g  a  d  r  e  t  a  z  o  s  j  f  u  f  v
a  j  t  g  i  z  r  e  b  o  t  k  o  s  g  e  k
n  z  r  e  t  n  e  l  e  g  e  h  s  f  f  c
p  n  o  w  s  g  z  t  i  e  m  c  f  j  u  l  i
s  c  l  m  b  t  z  e  g  a  d  s  n  i  d  v  b
b  s  i  v  e  e  r  e  b  m  e  t  p  e  s  a  n
t  r  a  a  m  r  f  h  s  g  a  d  n  a  a  m  d
m  n  u  z  a  e  m  e  s  p  n  o  z  i  e  s  z
n  b  j  v  e  o  p  a  j  u  n  i  z  w  s  l  z
```

Word Search Solution #26

```
r  d  k  z  z  u  s  t  i  e  f  v  a  d  e  r  e
e  g  t  c  g  s  k  t  b  e  u  v  t  m  z  k  o
d  k  c  a  r  z  h  o  d  n  i  k  n  i  e  l  k
a  p  p  e  o  c  z  l  e  i  l  i  m  a  f  d  h
v  w  d  l  i  z  m  n  e  t  n  a  w  r  e  v  a
t  u  e  n  s  l  v  p  d  n  n  e  e  f  e  l  o
o  w  z  t  h  d  s  t  i  e  f  m  o  e  d  e  r
o  r  z  c  n  n  o  o  z  f  e  i  t  s  w  t  g
r  u  d  m  b  a  w  r  e  t  h  c  o  d  k  b  u
g  h  g  r  o  o  t  m  o  e  d  e  r  z  k  l  u
```

Word Search Solution #27

```
c z s u f i h f b m m r d r s e d
f f t e n r p p p o e f i v t c o
o f e m o e d e r m i i u k i h c
a n l r o r d l r a m w r m e t h
b b z e z e w o c m r z b d f g t
g a m d p o p o k p n k k l z e e
d e n u m r d m r a o u a s u n r
l d i o f b f a m i l i e c s o m
u v n e t n a w r e v z i k t t o
e b u z i f z o v z u s b z g e f
```

Word Search Solution #28

```
m m o z m h m c w s s e k u e n b
s a o p n f s t i e f m o e d e r
w e m t b h e f m o e d e r d t a
d t k z p i w b z p s n e e f n v
u n w a l p o i r e t h c o d a f
z a v i e t n a w r e v s t d w b
n t m t n w w g c w k i n e n r v
g a e t o n e g t h c e r h w e w
f t i t o o n e g t h c e p o v z
l d n g o l m n a m f n d l v m h
```

Word Search Solution #29

b	t	v	a	n	o	o	z	n	s	z	t	n	e	e	f	m
w	h	e	i	g	r	o	o	t	m	o	e	d	e	r	t	o
o	c	r	z	h	p	d	i	d	c	l	a	d	l	s	u	e
i	i	w	a	r	e	d	e	o	m	f	e	i	t	s	w	d
e	n	a	a	u	r	e	o	r	b	s	v	h	e	i	p	e
d	a	n	v	l	n	r	e	d	a	v	f	e	i	t	s	r
i	o	t	n	t	e	e	c	h	t	g	e	n	o	o	t	d
u	i	e	g	v	u	m	o	u	h	k	n	f	d	m	z	c
r	g	n	e	t	n	a	w	r	e	v	i	e	w	n	a	m
b	r	e	t	h	c	o	d	f	e	i	t	s	g	b	r	d

Word Search Solution #30

s	t	h	c	i	n	b	r	e	d	a	v	f	e	i	t	s
s	k	b	i	s	t	i	e	f	b	r	o	e	r	z	f	k
f	m	f	w	c	r	v	m	n	s	o	k	h	v	d	m	t
s	t	i	e	f	z	u	s	e	s	u	l	n	c	s	e	t
r	b	o	o	m	d	o	m	e	n	b	z	o	a	e	e	b
u	b	m	r	w	v	h	u	f	v	a	d	e	r	d	k	c
n	l	m	o	e	d	e	r	d	n	l	k	b	p	a	a	d
b	f	a	l	b	t	g	e	z	e	h	s	e	m	v	r	t
b	w	m	s	r	e	d	u	o	t	r	b	w	r	o	p	u
s	m	m	n	o	o	z	f	e	i	t	s	k	k	s	z	t

Word Search Solution #31

```
l e z g i t f j i v s d w f f t z
l c d r i e h o n d e r d d n c d
n v e e r t i g g s w d o r e i v
e t o e u w w t o g e t n i g m g
i n l v f l o c z v w z g e u i i
t f d r e d n o h t h c a s t g t
r n e i t r e d h f e f r n z n r
e f i j w u v c d d n e i r s e e
e r o n z c a e j n m w w v s m d
v v a w n l i u j z t l l t e n u
```

Word Search Solution #32

```
n r f z e f e v d v e e r t i g n
e t o r h d r e d n o h h f l e s
i z r d r e d n o h n e v e z t f
t s j w t w d z a e z j e z u a s
t n e g e n t i e n e l l n e c r
h f r e e l o m u r s n a z w h s
c l c z i t e l e d t u c g i t z
a f i s w r g r i z i v h f v i a
f u f e t s d j h s g e t g c g o
d n e i t r e d s n o m u w e e s
```

Word Search Solution #33

a	n	n	v	i	j	f	t	i	e	n	w	s	t	u	z	n
a	i	e	z	e	v	e	n	h	o	n	d	e	r	d	e	h
n	j	o	e	u	n	a	c	h	t	h	o	n	d	e	r	d
t	z	z	l	z	l	e	z	l	v	g	o	u	z	e	c	
a	w	v	w	v	z	h	o	i	i	c	r	e	g	r	h	j
l	g	i	t	r	e	e	v	j	t	h	v	r	t	o	i	g
s	w	l	r	f	z	c	f	s	l	r	g	i	t	s	e	z
v	t	w	a	a	l	f	c	g	i	i	g	r	c	u	s	v
c	z	e	s	t	i	e	n	m	n	l	m	r	m	l	m	i
u	d	v	e	e	r	t	i	e	n	g	a	t	a	a	d	t

Word Search Solution #34

r	g	a	r	a	t	s	n	j	r	w	e	s	v	j	d	n
f	i	z	f	g	i	d	e	t	n	u	l	v	n	h	w	e
l	t	z	t	t	e	d	i	a	t	r	g	n	s	r	n	i
a	r	l	c	a	n	n	t	c	z	o	m	e	u	e	h	t
a	e	f	l	e	n	m	f	h	j	e	l	i	e	a	c	n
w	e	i	z	e	e	r	j	t	j	e	m	t	e	l	f	e
t	v	i	u	u	w	c	i	i	e	w	m	r	r	m	e	v
a	u	n	m	c	u	z	v	g	s	t	r	e	h	n	t	e
d	r	e	d	n	o	h	n	e	g	e	n	e	l	j	z	z
g	u	l	i	h	o	n	d	e	r	d	u	v	g	v	u	e

Word Search Solution #35

w	n	g	h	t	l	o	g	h	u	c	d	w	l	e	t	f
f	r	g	u	t	g	j	c	o	s	**n**	**e**	**i**	**t**	**r**	**e**	**d**
i	**n**	**e**	**i**	**t**	**t**	**h**	**c**	**a**	**g**	**i**	**t**	**r**	**e**	**e**	**v**	d
n	g	m	c	**n**	**e**	**g**	**e**	**n**	**h**	**o**	**n**	**d**	**e**	**r**	**d**	s
c	**h**	**n**	**e**	**o**	**j**	**l**	**i**	**m**	**z**	**e**	**v**	**e**	**n**	**t**	**i**	**g**
r	t	d	**s**	**e**	**z**	**n**	**e**	**i**	**t**	**n**	**e**	**v**	**e**	**z**	j	l
r	w	n	**f**	**l**	**e**	**t**	**w**	**e**	**e**	**h**	**o**	**n**	**d**	**e**	**r**	**d**
m	e	n	i	v	**g**	**i**	**t**	**s**	**e**	**z**	n	e	e	w	u	v
g	m	**g**	**i**	**t**	**h**	**c**	**a**	**t**	**g**	**i**	**t**	**n**	**i**	**w**	**t**	f
e	u	u	a	**h**	**o**	**n**	**d**	**e**	**r**	**d**	a	o	e	i	j	n

Word Search Solution #36

r	u	u	m	t	z	l	**r**	g	**l**	j	r	m	k	g	h	r
c	d	e	e	e	t	**a**	r	u	**e**	**t**	g	u	t	z	s	j
g	m	i	**k**	**a**	**a**	**k**	l	p	**v**	i	**s**	o	**d**	**n**	**a**	**h**
m	b	m	l	**h**	i	g	a	z	**e**	z	e	**r**	j	c	g	m
t	**b**	**l**	**i**	**n**	**d**	**e**	**d**	**a**	**r**	**m**	**g**	**e**	**o**	r	h	p
b	n	r	**k**	**l**	**i**	**e**	**r**	v	t	**n**	**l**	h	i	**b**	g	u
s	**j**	l	i	a	k	u	s	p	**o**	l	u	**r**	**e**	**d**	**a**	a
s	**i**	n	p	m	h	b	e	**t**	**i**	r	j	c	e	u	d	c
d	**d**	**l**	**e**	**k**	**n**	**e**	o	**a**	v	f	e	o	**s**	**l**	**o**	**p**
n	z	i	i	s	b	v	**t**	v	g	**h**	**e**	**u**	**p**	l	u	z

Word Search Solution #37

```
j k l l i g a s f w t h s m i z m
l a o g r d f o o h m t l m f n l
c m o z i n e t c r p e e t w e u
o v r i s s z p b z m o d e r d k
p w k c p o l s j p r v d u g n l
t h c i r w e g e e m b g r u a j
v d e m o j f e i i r h j l a t p
u u c p p o s n t w a l m a l a a
k i h e b i g f e u a k g k e n b
w m d m f f n j i r z d b h k m l
```

Word Search Solution #38

```
n b a a r d k k l i e r w a n g t
v b i i u i t o v h n j c d o b r
p i i f i u z r b z k d z b k s e
t s i u v s k g a h e i f v p w d
m r f j t b i w c h l n u m o z u
o b n e r s z w g a a m u b j i o
n t e r e v e l f t u b s j d z h
d n r t t n b r v e u s k l c j c
f j j k u n c o w t b c r i d a s
p i l o m f w d s l r h j c g u r
```

147

Word Search Solution #39

```
m b l i n d e d a r m l e k n e r
u r n w z i t v b z r m n n c k t
n r k k m z h f b j r g d v r u h
e a g b o t c o o i i u m b e g h
t a b b k v i t r d i v i i l d t
e e o u m s z m s m z d b r v a b
o p n n i k e i t c p u e h i r r
r a g z g k g e k a n t f l h f k
p i h k m c o k a a k o l b h w r
s p t e o v u f s m n e o j i o f
```

Word Search Solution #40

```
r b i t a j h d z s a k t s r o b
w e l l i a t g d z u n p t c v s
o h z t u i d i u l v o e t e n f
o n e i o n b a e r k n o k k e l
i s g t i n p n h a w o w v o v v
k u r k g r g n h h e r s e n e n
a m c v v l r e d a g a l s o i r
p u o t h c i z e g p o l s s u i
i i s n t h c w n l f j c g w o b
i e n z d v l e g a n r e g n i v
```

148

Word Scramble Hints

#1 - 1) jaguar   2) leopard   3) porcupine   4) crocodile
5) anteater   6) pig   7) lamb

#2 - 1) panther   2) hyena   3) toad   4) zebra   5) elephant
6) rabbit   7) chipmunk

#3 - 1) koala   2) rhinoceros   3) llama   4) squirrel   5) badger
6) bear   7) goat

#4 - 1) frog   2) hippopotamus   3) baboon   4) hyena
5) buffalo   6) panther   7) lynx

#5 - 1) chipmunk   2) panther   3) sheep   4) lamb   5) camel
6) rhinoceros   7) hyena

#6 - 1) kettle   2) soap   3) vase   4) tap   5) napkin   6) drawer
7) kitchen

#7 - 1) torch   2) wall   3) sheet   4) ashtray   5) mirror
6) dishwasher   7) soap

#8 - 1) image   2) chair   3) switch   4) loo   5) napkin
6) telephone   7) box

#9 - 1) pillow   2) bag   3) rubbish can   4) glass   5) hoover
6) knife   7) dresser

#10 - 1) purse   2) clock   3) bed   4) pot   5) wall   6) shower
7) handbag

Word Scramble Hints

#11 - 1) size   2) zip   3) bathing suit   4) hiking boots   5) bow tie   6) tights   7) coat

#12 - 1) coat   2) slippers   3) jumper   4) dress   5) corset   6) knickers   7) T-shirt

#13 - 1) skirt   2) jacket   3) size   4) overcoat   5) belt   6) glove   7) dress

#14 - 1) suit   2) sandals   3) dress   4) bikini   5) socks   6) hat   7) handkerchief

#15 - 1) cardigan   2) necktie   3) blouse   4) bathing suit   5) scarf   6) overcoat   7) knickers

#16 - 1) blue   2) white   3) colour   4) dark   5) green   6) brown   7) red

#17 - 1) red   2) yellow   3) orange   4) brown   5) grey   6) black   7) colour

#18 - 1) maroon   2) pink   3) beige   4) blond   5) colour   6) orange   7) yellow

#19 - 1) pink   2) blue   3) yellow   4) blond   5) orange   6) white   7) maroon

#20 - 1) dark   2) pink   3) green   4) maroon   5) brown   6) white   7) beige

Word Scramble Hints

#21 - 1) Wednesday 2) December 3) January 4) February
5) Thursday 6) summer 7) October

#22 - 1) November 2) month 3) September 4) Tuesday
5) April 6) Sunday 7) March

#23 - 1) September 2) November 3) January 4) June
5) May 6) Monday 7) Sunday

#24 - 1) month 2) summer 3) Friday 4) spring 5) day
6) Wednesday 7) July

#25 - 1) Tuesday 2) autumn 3) September 4) Wednesday
5) April 6) July 7) Saturday

#26 - 1) niece 2) son 3) stepbrother 4) parents 5) mother
6) husband 7) nephew

#27 - 1) grandchild 2) grandmother 3) uncle 4) parent
5) son 6) niece 7) relative

#28 - 1) parents 2) stepdaughter 3) daughter 4) dad
5) grandchild 6) sister 7) father

#29 - 1) aunt 2) son 3) stepsister 4) dad 5) parent
6) mum 7) family

#30 - 1) uncle 2) relative 3) family 4) niece 5) nephew
6) stepbrother 7) wife

Word Scramble Hints

#31 - 1) four   2) fourteen   3) two hundred   4) fifteen   5) one billion   6) number   7) nineteen

#32 - 1) one billion   2) seventeen   3) fifty   4) one million   5) eight hundred   6) five   7) seven hundred

#33 - 1) sixty   2) eight hundred   3) three   4) one billion   5) seventeen   6) two hundred   7) ninety

#34 - 1) fourteen   2) twelve   3) one million   4) seventy   5) six   6) seven   7) four

#35 - 1) twenty   2) one billion   3) number   4) three hundred   5) eighty   6) forty   7) seven

#36 - 1) muscle   2) thumb   3) back   4) face   5) appendix   6) toe   7) blood

#37 - 1) ankle   2) thorax   3) artery   4) feet   5) back   6) lip   7) muscle

#38 - 1) beard   2) eyelid   3) eyelash   4) jaw   5) brain   6) gland   7) teeth

#39 - 1) appendix   2) face   3) heart   4) eyelid   5) wrist   6) iris   7) knee

#40 - 1) backbone   2) elbow   3) vein   4) ankle   5) kidney   6) freckles   7) appendix

Word Scramble Solutions

#1 - 1) jaguar   2) luipaard   3) stekelvarken   4) krokodil
5) miereneter   6) varken   7) lam

#2 - 1) panter   2) hyena   3) pad   4) zebra   5) olifant
6) konijn   7) wangzakeekhoorn

#3 - 1) koala   2) neushoorn   3) lama   4) stinkdier   5) das
6) beer   7) geit

#4 - 1) kikker   2) nijlpaard   3) baviaan   4) hyena   5) buffel
6) panter   7) lynx

#5 - 1) wangzakeekhoorn   2) panter   3) schaap   4) lam
5) kameel   6) neushoorn   7) hyena

#6 - 1) ketel   2) zeep   3) vaas   4) kraan   5) tafellaken
6) lade   7) keuken

#7 - 1) zaklamp   2) muur   3) laken   4) asbak   5) spiegel
6) vaatwasmachine   7) zeep

#8 - 1) beeld   2) stoel   3) schakelaar   4) badkamer
5) tafellaken   6) telefoon   7) doos

#9 - 1) slaapkussen   2) zak   3) vuilnisbak   4) glas
5) stofzuiger   6) mes   7) ladekast

#10 - 1) portemonnee   2) klok   3) bed   4) pot   5) muur
6) douche   7) handtas

Word Scramble Solutions

#11 - 1) grootte   2) rits   3) badpak   4) wandelschoenen
 5) vlinderdas   6) maillot   7) jas

#12 - 1) jas   2) slippers   3) trui   4) jurk   5) korset   6) slipje
 7) t-shirt

#13 - 1) rok   2) jas   3) grootte   4) overjas   5) riem
 6) handschoen   7) jurk

#14 - 1) pak   2) sandalen   3) jurk   4) bikini   5) sokken
 6) hoed   7) zakdoek

#15 - 1) vest   2) stropdas   3) bloes   4) badpak   5) sjaal
 6) overjas   7) slipje

#16 - 1) blauw   2) wit   3) kleur   4) donker   5) groen
 6) bruin   7) rood

#17 - 1) rood   2) geel   3) oranje   4) bruin   5) grijs   6) zwart
 7) kleur

#18 - 1) donkerbruin   2) roze   3) beige   4) blond   5) kleur
 6) oranje   7) geel

#19 - 1) roze   2) blauw   3) geel   4) blond   5) oranje   6) wit
 7) donkerbruin

#20 - 1) donker   2) roze   3) groen   4) donkerbruin   5) bruin
 6) wit   7) beige

Word Scramble Solutions

#21 - 1) woensdag   2) december   3) januari   4) februari
5) donderdag   6) zomer   7) oktober

#22 - 1) november   2) maand   3) september   4) dinsdag
5) april   6) zondag   7) maart

#23 - 1) september   2) november   3) januari   4) juni   5) mei
6) maandag   7) zondag

#24 - 1) maand   2) zomer   3) vrijdag   4) lente   5) dag
6) woensdag   7) juli

#25 - 1) dinsdag   2) herfst   3) september   4) woensdag
5) april   6) juli   7) zaterdag

#26 - 1) nicht   2) zoon   3) stiefbroer   4) ouders   5) moeder
6) echtgenoot   7) neef

#27 - 1) kleinkind   2) grootmoeder   3) oom   4) ouder
5) zoon   6) nicht   7) verwante

#28 - 1) ouders   2) stiefdochter   3) dochter   4) pa
5) kleinkind   6) zus   7) vader

#29 - 1) tante   2) zoon   3) stiefzus   4) pa   5) ouder   6) ma
7) familie

#30 - 1) oom   2) verwante   3) familie   4) nicht   5) neef
6) stiefbroer   7) echtgenote

Word Scramble Solutions

#31 - 1) vier 2) veertien 3) tweehonderd 4) vijftien
5) miljard 6) aantal 7) negentien

#32 - 1) miljard 2) zeventien 3) vijftig 4) miljoen
5) achthonderd 6) vijf 7) zevenhonderd

#33 - 1) zestig 2) achthonderd 3) drie 4) miljard
5) zeventien 6) tweehonderd 7) negentig

#34 - 1) veertien 2) twaalf 3) miljoen 4) zeventig 5) zes
6) zeven 7) vier

#35 - 1) twintig 2) miljard 3) aantal 4) driehonderd
5) tachtig 6) veertig 7) zeven

#36 - 1) spier 2) duim 3) rug 4) gezicht 5) blindedarm
6) teen 7) bloed

#37 - 1) enkel 2) borstkas 3) slagader 4) voeten 5) rug
6) lip 7) spier

#38 - 1) baard 2) ooglid 3) wimper 4) kaak 5) hersenen
6) klier 7) tanden

#39 - 1) blindedarm 2) gezicht 3) hart 4) ooglid 5) pols
6) iris 7) knie

#40 - 1) ruggengraat 2) elleboog 3) ader 4) enkel 5) nier
6) sproeten 7) blindedarm

Word Quiz Solutions

#1 - 1) c - squirrel   2) d - frog   3) c - zebra   4) b - cow
 5) a - bull   6) c - beaver   7) a - porcupine   8) c - crocodile
 9) b - rhinoceros   10) a - monkey

#2 - 1) c - lamb   2) c - lynx   3) d - zebra   4) b - elephant
 5) a - sheep   6) a - dog   7) c - jaguar   8) b - horse
 9) a - squirrel   10) c - kangaroo

#3 - 1) b - baboon   2) a - dog   3) b - koala   4) b - rabbit
 5) b - wolf   6) c - mouse   7) d - cat   8) a - anteater
 9) c - lion   10) a - chipmunk

#4 - 1) a - panter   2) b - lama   3) b - pad   4) d - olifant
 5) b - hyena   6) c - koe   7) a - gordeldier   8) a - miereneter
 9) a - paard   10) b - aardvarken

#5 - 1) b - rat   2) c - aardvarken   3) c - hyena
 4) c - luipaard   5) d - ezel   6) b - paard   7) a - schaap
 8) c - krokodil   9) b - kikker   10) a - jaguar

#6 - 1) a - television   2) c - table   3) a - rubbish bag
 4) b - ceiling   5) b - alarm clock   6) d - purse   7) c - picture
 8) d - sheet   9) a - switch   10) b - kitchen

#7 - 1) b - washing machine   2) a - freezer   3) a - bath (tub)
 4) b - roof   5) d - bowl   6) b - plate   7) a - radio   8) b - key
 9) b - mixer   10) b - ashtray

Word Quiz Solutions

#8 - 1) b - glass   2) b - purse   3) a - bath (tub)   4) c - torch
5) b - vase   6) a - hoover   7) b - ceiling   8) d - roof
9) c - wardrobe   10) a - bed

#9 - 1) d - portemonnee   2) d - schotel
3) c - vaatwasmachine   4) b - schilderij   5) d - badkuip
6) a - mixer   7) b - broodrooster   8) a - handtas   9) c - beeld
10) d - kast

#10 - 1) b - tafel   2) d - mixer   3) c - lepel   4) b - douche
5) d - stoel   6) a - plafond   7) b - asbak   8) d - zaklamp
9) c - braadpan   10) d - droger

#11 - 1) a - running shoes   2) b - pyjamas   3) a - suit
4) d - jeans   5) c - bathing suit   6) c - hiking boots
7) b - briefs   8) a - corset   9) a - cardigan   10) a - umbrella

#12 - 1) d - size   2) a - shirt   3) c - socks   4) c - jumper
5) c - scarf   6) a - dress   7) a - tights   8) b - bow tie
9) c - zip   10) c - suit

#13 - 1) d - clothes   2) d - jeans   3) d - blouse
4) b - pyjamas   5) d - bikini   6) d - socks   7) a - scarf
8) c - jumpsuit   9) c - bathing suit   10) d - hiking boots

#14 - 1) d - pet   2) a - overall   3) b - sandalen   4) a - jas
5) b - pantalon   6) a - sjaal   7) c - badjas   8) c - kousen
9) c - t-shirt   10) b - hemd

Word Quiz Solutions

#15 - 1) b - overjas   2) b - korset   3) a - slippers
 4) c - spijkerbroek   5) b - wandelschoenen
 6) c - onderbroek   7) a - pak   8) d - rits   9) c - jurk
 10) a - zakdoek

#16 - 1) a - dark   2) c - pink   3) b - brown   4) a - purple
 5) d - blond   6) d - beige   7) d - colour   8) d - green
 9) c - bright   10) a - grey

#17 - 1) d - beige   2) c - grey   3) c - brown   4) d - maroon
 5) a - green   6) d - white   7) c - yellow   8) b - blond
 9) c - purple   10) c - dark

#18 - 1) d - purple   2) c - blond   3) d - green   4) c - maroon
 5) a - grey   6) c - black   7) b - beige   8) a - dark
 9) a - orange   10) a - brown

#19 - 1) c - donkerbruin   2) a - blond   3) b - donker
 4) d - wit   5) c - oranje   6) a - geel   7) d - rood
 8) c - groen   9) c - kleur   10) c - beige

#20 - 1) d - donker   2) a - blond   3) b - kleur   4) b - bruin
 5) d - rood   6) c - zwart   7) c - wit   8) c - geel   9) a - grijs
 10) d - blauw

#21 - 1) b - Monday   2) b - Thursday   3) c - August
 4) a - Friday   5) d - Saturday   6) b - Sunday   7) d - summer
 8) c - autumn   9) d - winter   10) d - Tuesday

Word Quiz Solutions

#22 - 1) a - April   2) a - summer   3) c - winter
 4) b - December   5) c - March   6) b - spring   7) d - January
 8) b - season   9) a - May   10) b - June

#23 - 1) b - month   2) d - February   3) d - Friday
 4) a - September   5) a - winter   6) d - November
 7) a - Thursday   8) d - June   9) a - October
 10) a - Saturday

#24 - 1) c - april   2) d - dinsdag   3) d - dag   4) b - februari
 5) b - woensdag   6) b - januari   7) c - juni   8) c - maart
 9) d - seizon   10) b - lente

#25 - 1) c - lente   2) b - maand   3) d - februari
 4) a - zondag   5) c - november   6) b - seizon
 7) b - augustus   8) a - mei   9) b - woensdag   10) c - winter

#26 - 1) c - bride   2) b - stepsister   3) d - aunt   4) b - cousin
 5) a - uncle   6) c - dad   7) c - daughter   8) d - wife
 9) a - sister   10) a - father

#27 - 1) b - husband   2) c - grandfather   3) d - grandmother
 4) c - dad   5) b - parents   6) b - son   7) c - stepson
 8) a - wife   9) a - brother   10) c - uncle

#28 - 1) a - parent   2) b - brother   3) a - stepdaughter
 4) b - sister   5) c - nephew   6) d - husband   7) b - mother
 8) a - aunt   9) b - bride   10) a - grandfather

Word Quiz Solutions

#29 - 1) d - broer   2) c - nicht   3) c - verwante   4) a - ma
5) a - zoon   6) d - zus   7) c - stiefzus   8) b - echtgenote
9) c - moeder   10) c - verwanten

#30 - 1) d - oom   2) c - neef   3) c - zus   4) b - nicht
5) d - bruid   6) d - grootvader   7) a - ouder   8) b - zoon
9) c - neef   10) d - dochter

#31 - 1) b - one thousand   2) a - zero   3) c - ten   4) b - two
hundred   5) d - eleven   6) c - eight   7) a - six hundred
8) a - eighteen   9) b - seven   10) b - number

#32 - 1) d - twenty   2) b - seventy   3) a - number   4) c - fifty
5) b - forty   6) d - three hundred   7) b - seven hundred
8) d - seven   9) c - three   10) b - nineteen

#33 - 1) d - one million   2) d - one hundred   3) d - two
4) c - sixty   5) a - zero   6) c - fifteen   7) d - seventeen
8) a - eighty   9) c - four   10) b - nineteen

#34 - 1) d - tachtig   2) c - veertien   3) d - zes   4) b - dertig
5) a - zestig   6) d - acht   7) c - tien   8) a - achttien
9) a - vierhonderd   10) b - duizend

#35 - 1) c - zes   2) c - duizend   3) c - achttien
4) d - tweehonderd   5) a - miljoen   6) d - vijfhonderd
7) d - zevenhonderd   8) a - veertig   9) d - negentien
10) c - tien

Word Quiz Solutions

#36 - 1) c - back   2) a - body   3) b - backbone   4) d - knee
5) d - artery   6) b - eyelid   7) c - stomach   8) b - waist
9) d - wrist   10) a - moustache

#37 - 1) a - blood   2) c - teeth   3) a - fingernail   4) b - feet
5) c - liver   6) c - finger   7) c - ear   8) a - stomach
9) c - bladder   10) c - thigh

#38 - 1) c - hair   2) d - foot   3) b - iris   4) d - breast
5) a - brain   6) d - mouth   7) b - artery   8) a - leg
9) d - finger   10) c - heart

#39 - 1) b - keel   2) d - bot   3) c - nek   4) d - buik   5) b - dij
6) b - wimper   7) a - kin   8) d - amandelen   9) b - enkel
10) a - hand

#40 - 1) a - voeten   2) d - borst   3) c - been   4) c - ooglid
5) d - ader   6) b - tong   7) d - lip   8) a - klier   9) b - dij
10) b - vingernagel

Welcome to the Dictionary section!

Dutch words are given in bold, with the English meaning after.

Definite articles are given in ().

Parts of speech are given in [].

m = masculine noun

f = feminine noun

mf = masculine / feminine noun

n = neuter noun

adj = adjective

num = number

mp = masculine plural

fp = feminine plural

mfp = masculine / feminine plural

np = neuter plural

adv = adverb

v = verb

aantal (het) *[n]* - number
aap (de) *[m]* - monkey
aardvarken (het) *[n]* - aardvark
acht *[num]* - eight
achthonderd *[num]* - eight hundred
achttien *[num]* - eighteen
ader (de) *[m]* - vein
alligator (de) *[m]* - alligator
amandelen (de) *[fp]* - tonsils
april *[f]* - April
arm (de) *[m]* - arm
asbak (de) *[m]* - ashtray
augustus *[m]* - August
baard (de) *[m]* - beard
badjas (de) *[f]* - dressing gown
badkamer (de) *[m]* - loo
badkuip (de) *[m]* - bath (tub)
badpak (het) *[n]* - bathing suit
bank (de) *[m]* - couch
baviaan (de) *[m]* - baboon
bed (het) *[n]* - bed
beeld (het) *[n]* - image
been (het) *[n]* - leg
beer (de) *[m]* - bear
beha (de) *[m]* - bra
beige *[adj]* - beige
bever (de) *[m]* - beaver
bezem (de) *[m]* - broom
bikini (de) *[m]* - bikini
blaas (de) *[n]* - bladder
blauw *[adj]* - blue
blik (het) *[n]* - tin
blindedarm (de) *[n]* - appendix
bloed (het) *[n]* - blood
bloes (de) *[f]* - blouse

blond *[adj]* - blond
boekenkast (de) *[m]* - bookcase
borst (de) *[n]* - breast
borstkas (de) *[f]* - thorax
bot (het) *[n]* - bone
braadpan (de) *[f]* - frying pan
broer (de) *[m]* - brother
broodrooster (de) *[m]* - toaster
bruid (de) *[f]* - bride
bruin *[adj]* - brown
buffel (de) *[m]* - buffalo
buik (de) *[m]* - belly
dag (de) *[m]* - day
dak (het) *[n]* - roof
das (de) *[m]* - badger
december *[m]* - December
deken (het) *[n]* - blanket
dertien *[num]* - thirteen
dertig *[num]* - thirty
deur (de) *[m]* - door
diepvriezer (de) *[m]* - freezer
dier (het) *[n]* - animal
dij (de) *[f]* - thigh
dinsdag (de) *[m]* - Tuesday
dochter (de) *[f]* - daughter
donderdag (de) *[m]* - Thursday
donker *[adj]* - dark
donkerbruin *[adj]* - maroon
doos (de) *[m]* - box
douche (de) *[m]* - shower
douchegordijn (het) *[n]* - shower curtain
drie *[num]* - three
driehonderd *[num]* - three hundred
drinkglas (het) *[n]* - drinking glass
droger (de) *[m]* - drier
duim (de) *[m]* - thumb

duizend *[num]* - one thousand
echtgenoot (de) *[m]* - husband
echtgenote (de) *[f]* - wife
een *[num]* - one
elf *[num]* - eleven
elleboog (de) *[m]* - elbow
enkel (de) *[m]* - ankle
ezel (de) *[m]* - donkey
familie (de) *[f]* - family
februari *[m]* - February
fles (de) *[f]* - bottle
gazelle (de) *[f]* - gazelle
geel *[adj]* - yellow
geit (de) *[m]* - goat
gewricht (het) *[n]* - joint
gezicht (het) *[n]* - face
giraffe (de) *[f]* - giraffe
glas (het) *[n]* - glass
gordeldier (het) *[n]* - armadillo
gordijn (het) *[n]* - curtain
gorilla (de) *[m]* - gorilla
grijs *[adj]* - grey
groen *[adj]* - green
grootmoeder (de) *[f]* - grandmother
grootte (de) *[f]* - size
grootvader (de) *[m]* - grandfather
haar (het) *[n]* - hair
hand (de) *[n]* - hand
handschoen (de) *[m]* - glove
handschoenen (de) *[m]* - gloves
handtas (de) *[f]* - handbag
hart (het) *[n]* - heart
helder *[adj]* - bright
hemd (het) *[n]* - shirt
herfst (de) *[m]* - autumn
hersenen (de) *[f]* - brain

hert (het) *[n]* - deer
heup (de) *[f]* - hip
hoed (de) *[m]* - hat
hond (de) *[m]* - dog
honderd *[num]* - one hundred
hoofd (het) *[n]* - head
huid (de) *[n]* - skin
huis (het) *[n]* - house
hyena (de) *[m]* - hyena
iris (de) *[f]* - iris
jachtluipaard (het) *[n]* - cheetah
jaguar (de) *[m]* - jaguar
januari *[m]* - January
jas (de) *[m]* - jacket
jas (de) *[f]* - coat
juli *[m]* - July
juni *[m]* - June
jurk (de) *[m]* - dress
kaak (de) *[f]* - jaw
kachel (de) *[m]* - stove
kameel (de) *[m]* - camel
kangoeroe (de) *[m]* - kangaroo
kast (de) *[m]* - cabinet
kat (de) *[m]* - cat
keel (de) *[m]* - throat
ketel (de) *[m]* - kettle
keuken (de) *[f]* - kitchen
kikker (de) *[m]* - frog
kin (de) *[n]* - chin
kledingkast (de) *[m]* - wardrobe
kleinkind (het) *[n]* - grandchild
kleren (de) *[f]* - clothes
kleur (de) *[m]* - colour
klier (de) *[n]* - gland
klok (de) *[m]* - clock
knie (de) *[f]* - knee

knokkel (de) *[m]* - knuckle
koala (de) *[m]* - koala
koe (de) *[f]* - cow
koelkast (de) *[m]* - refrigerator
koffiepot (de) *[m]* - coffee pot
kom (de) *[m]* - bowl
konijn (het) *[n]* - rabbit
kop (de) *[m]* - cup
korset (het) *[n]* - corset
kousen (de) *[mf]* - stockings
kraan (de) *[m]* - tap
krokodil (de) *[m]* - crocodile
lade (de) *[m]* - drawer
ladekast (de) *[m]* - dresser
laken (het) *[n]* - sheet
lam (het) *[n]* - lamb
lama (de) *[m]* - llama
lamp (de) *[f]* - lamp
leeuw (de) *[m]* - lion
lente (de) *[f]* - spring
lepel (de) *[m]* - spoon
lever (de) *[n]* - liver
lichaam (het) *[n]* - body
lichaamsdelen (de) *[mp]* - parts of the body
lip (de) *[n]* - lip
long (de) *[f]* - lung
luipaard (het) *[n]* - leopard
lynx (de) *[m]* - lynx
ma (de) *[f]* - mum
maag (de) *[n]* - stomach
maand (de) *[f]* - month
maandag (de) *[m]* - Monday
maart *[m]* - March
maillot (de) *[m]* - tights
mei *[m]* - May
mes (het) *[n]* - knife

meubilair (het) *[n]* - furniture
miereneter (de) *[m]* - anteater
miljard *[num]* - one billion
miljoen *[num]* - one million
mixer (de) *[m]* - mixer
moeder (de) *[f]* - mother
mond (de) *[m]* - mouth
muilezel (de) *[m]* - mule
muis (de) *[f]* - mouse
muur (de) *[m]* - wall
neef (de) *[m]* - cousin, nephew
negen *[num]* - nine
negenhonderd *[num]* - nine hundred
negentien *[num]* - nineteen
negentig *[num]* - ninety
nek (de) *[m]* - neck
neus (de) *[m]* - nose
neushoorn (de) *[m]* - rhinoceros
nicht (de) *[f]* - niece
nier (de) *[n]* - kidney
nijlpaard (het) *[n]* - hippopotamus
november *[m]* - November
nul *[num]* - zero
oktober *[m]* - October
olifant (de) *[m]* - elephant
onderbroek (de) *[m]* - briefs
oog (het) *[n]* - eye
ooglid (het) *[n]* - eyelid
oom (de) *[m]* - uncle
oor (het) *[n]* - ear
oranje *[adj]* - orange
ouder (de) *[f]* - parent
ouders (de) *[f]* - parents
overall (de) *[m]* - overalls
overjas (de) *[m]* - overcoat
pa (de) *[m]* - dad

paard (het) *[n]* - horse
paars *[adj]* - purple
pad (de) *[m]* - toad
pak (het) *[n]* - suit
panda (de) *[m]* - panda
pantalon (de) *[m]* - trousers
panter (de) *[m]* - panther
paraplu (de) *[f]* - umbrella
pees (de) *[n]* - tendon
pet (de) *[m]* - cap
plaatje (het) *[n]* - picture
plafond (het) *[n]* - ceiling
plank (de) *[m]* - shelf
poema (de) *[m]* - cougar
pols (de) *[m]* - wrist
portemonnee (de) *[m]* - purse, wallet
pot (de) *[m]* - pot
pyjama (de) *[m]* - pyjamas
raam (het) *[n]* - window
radio (de) *[m]* - radio
rat (de) *[m]* - rat
rib (de) *[n]* - rib
riem (de) *[m]* - belt
rits (de) *[m]* - zip
rode lynx (de) *[m]* - bobcat
rok (de) *[m]* - skirt
rood *[adj]* - red
roze *[adj]* - pink
rug (de) *[n]* - back
ruggengraat (de) *[m]* - backbone
sandalen (de) *[m]* - sandals
schaal (de) *[m]* - plate
schaap (het) *[n]* - sheep
schakelaar (de) *[m]* - switch
schilderij (het) *[n]* - painting
schildpad (de) *[m]* - tortoise

schotel (de) *[m]* - dish
schouder (de) *[m]* - shoulder
seizon (het) *[n]* - season
september *[m]* - September
sjaal (de) *[m]* - scarf
slaapkussen (het) *[n]* - pillow
slaapzak (de) *[m]* - sleeping bag
slagader (de) *[m]* - artery
slang (de) *[m]* - snake
sleutel (de) *[m]* - key
slipje (het) *[n]* - knickers
slippers (de) *[m]* - slippers
snor (de) *[m]* - moustache
sokken (de) *[m]* - socks
spiegel (de) *[m]* - mirror
spier (de) *[n]* - muscle
spijkerbroek (de) *[m]* - jeans
sportschoenen (de) *[m]* - running shoes
sproeten (de) *[mp]* - freckles
stekelvarken (het) *[n]* - porcupine
stiefbroer (de) *[m]* - stepbrother
stiefdochter (de) *[f]* - stepdaughter
stiefmoeder (de) *[f]* - stepmother
stiefvader (de) *[m]* - stepfather
stiefzoon (de) *[m]* - stepson
stiefzus (de) *[f]* - stepsister
stier (de) *[m]* - bull
stinkdier (het) *[n]* - squirrel
stoel (de) *[m]* - chair
stofzuiger (de) *[m]* - hoover
stropdas (de) *[m]* - necktie
t-shirt (het) *[n]* - T-shirt
tachtig *[num]* - eighty
tafel (de) *[f]* - table
tafellaken (het) *[n]* - napkin
taille (de) *[n]* - waist

tand (de) *[m]* - tooth
tanden (de) *[mp]* - teeth
tante (de) *[f]* - aunt
tapijt (het) *[n]* - carpet
teen (de) *[m]* - toe
telefoon (de) *[m]* - telephone
televisie (de) *[f]* - television
tien *[num]* - ten
tijger (de) *[m]* - tiger
toilet (het) *[n]* - toilet
tong (de) *[n]* - tongue
trap (de) *[f]* - staircase
trui (de) *[m]* - jumper, sweatshirt
twaalf *[num]* - twelve
twee *[num]* - two
tweehonderd *[num]* - two hundred
twintig *[num]* - twenty
uniform (het) *[n]* - jumpsuit
vaas (de) *[f]* - vase
vaatwasmachine (de) *[m]* - dishwasher
vader (de) *[m]* - father
varken (het) *[n]* - pig
vat (het) *[n]* - pail
veertien *[num]* - fourteen
veertig *[num]* - forty
verwante (de) *[m]* - relative
verwanten (de) *[m]* - relatives
vest (het) *[n]* - cardigan, waistcoat
vier *[num]* - four
vierhonderd *[num]* - four hundred
vijf *[num]* - five
vijfhonderd *[num]* - five hundred
vijftien *[num]* - fifteen
vijftig *[num]* - fifty
vinger (de) *[m]* - finger
vingernagel (de) *[m]* - fingernail

173

vlinderdas (de) *[m]* - bow tie
vloer (de) *[m]* - floor
voet (de) *[m]* - foot
voeten (de) *[mp]* - feet
voorhoofd (het) *[n]* - forehead
vork (de) *[m]* - fork
vos (de) *[m]* - fox
vrijdag (de) *[m]* - Friday
vuilnisbak (de) *[m]* - rubbish can
vuilniszak (de) *[m]* - rubbish bag
vuist (de) *[n]* - fist
wandelschoenen (de) *[m]* - hiking boots
wang (de) *[f]* - cheek
wangzakeekhoorn (de) *[m]* - chipmunk
wasmachine (de) *[f]* - washing machine
water (het) *[n]* - water
wekker (de) *[m]* - alarm clock
wenkbrauw (de) *[m]* - eyebrow
wimper (de) *[m]* - eyelash
winter (de) *[m]* - winter
wit *[adj]* - white
woensdag (de) *[m]* - Wednesday
wolf (de) *[m]* - wolf
zak (de) *[m]* - bag
zakdoek (de) *[m]* - handkerchief
zaklamp (de) *[f]* - torch
zaterdag (de) *[m]* - Saturday
zebra (de) *[m]* - zebra
zeep (de) *[f]* - soap
zenuw (de) *[n]* - nerve
zes *[num]* - six
zeshonderd *[num]* - six hundred
zestien *[num]* - sixteen
zestig *[num]* - sixty
zeven *[num]* - seven
zevenhonderd *[num]* - seven hundred

zeventien *[num]* - seventeen
zeventig *[num]* - seventy
zomer (de) *[m]* - summer
zondag (de) *[m]* - Sunday
zoon (de) *[m]* - son
zus (de) *[f]* - sister
zwart *[adj]* - black

About the Author

Erik Zidowecki is a computer programmer and language lover. He is a co-founder of UniLang and founder of Parleremo, both web communities dedicated to helping people learn languages. He is also the Editor in Chief of Parrot Time magazine, a magazine devoted to language, linguistics, culture and the Parleremo community.

About Parleremo Languages

Parleremo is a language learning web site and online community. Free to any who wish to learn about languages and cultures, Parleremo uses a mixture of static and interactive resources as well as peer to peer sharing of knowledge and experience.

We are devoted to providing language materials and resources to people that want to learn and work with a like minded community.

Connect with Me:

Follow me on Twitter:
https://twitter.com/Parleremo
Friend me on Facebook:
https://www.facebook.com/ezidowecki
Join my group on Facebook:
https://www.facebook.com/groups/264839636895941/
Join my site: http://www.parleremo.org/